Cisco ASA Security Appliance Training
Student Exercise Manual Edition 2.1d

Author: Don R. Crawley, soundtraining.net

Software Version: 9.11 and 9.14

Copyright 2016, soundtraining.net. All rights reserved. It is illegal to make copies of this document in any form. www.soundtraining.net If you believe this is an illegal copy, please contact soundtraining.net at (206) 988-5858.

Special discounts are available on bulk quantities of soundtraining.net books. For details, contact soundtraining.net, a division of Crawley International, Inc., PO Box 48094, Seattle, WA 98148.

Telephone: (206) 988-5858

Email: info@soundtraining.net

Website: www.soundtraining.net

Cover design by Jason Sprenger, Fourth Cup Print and Web Design, Overland Park, Kansas

Reasonable attempts have been made to ensure the accuracy of the information contained in this publication as of the date on which it was written. This publication is distributed in the hope that it will be helpful, but with no guarantees. There are no guarantees made as to the accuracy, reliability, or applicability of this information for any task or purpose whatsoever.

The author recommends that these procedures be used only as a guide to configuration of computers and/or devices in a test environment prior to usage in a production environment. Under no circumstances should these procedures be used in a live, production environment without first being tested in a laboratory environment to determine their suitability, their accuracy, and any security implications.

ISBN: 978-0-9836607-8-1

© 2016, Don R. Crawley.
All rights reserved.

This is a copyrighted work in which all rights are retained by the author. You may not copy this work in any form, nor change this work, nor store this document in a retrieval system, nor distribute or otherwise transmit this work in any form by any means, electronic, mechanical, photocopying, recording, or otherwise, without the written prior permission of the copyright holder. The preceding restrictions apply to this document in whole or in part.

Trademarks, Registered Trademarks, and Service Marks: This book identifies and uses product names and services known to be trademarks, registered trademarks, or service marks of their respective holders. Such marks are used throughout this book in an editorial fashion only. Additionally, terms suspected of being trademarks, registered trademarks, or service marks have been appropriately capitalized, although soundtraining.net cannot attest to the accuracy of such information. Use of a term in this book should not be regarded as affecting the validity of any trademark, registered trademark, or service mark. Neither the author nor soundtraining.net are associated with any vendor or product mentioned in this book.

Please do not make illegal copies of this book, either in its entirety or any portion thereof.

soundtraining.net
learning resources for IT pros

PO Box 48094
Seattle, Washington 98148-0094
United States of America
On the web: www.soundtraining.net
On the phone: (206) 988-5858
Email: info@soundtraining.net

Copyright 2016, soundtraining.net. All rights reserved. It is illegal to make copies of this document in any form. www.soundtraining.net If you believe this is an illegal copy, please contact soundtraining.net at (206) 988-5858.

Table of Contents

Prerequisites for Successfully Using this Lab Manual 7
General Instructions for the Student 7
Hands-On Exercise 1.1: Password Recovery and Initial Configuration 9
    Hands-On Exercise 1.1.1: Connecting to the Security Appliance's Console Port 9
    Hands-On Exercise 1.1.2: Password Recovery on the Security Appliance 9
    For Your Information: Disallowing Password Recovery 11
Hands-On Exercise 1.2: Removing the Existing Configuration 12
Hands-On Exercise 1.3: Using the Eight Commands Required to Enable Basic Firewall Functionality 12
    Assign Interface Names, IP Addresses, and a Default Route 12
    Configure Port Address Translation 13
    Test the Configuration 13
Hands-On Exercise 1.4: Building a Base Configuration on the ASA Security Appliance 14
    Hands-On Exercise 1.4.1: Removing the Existing Configuration on Your Security Appliance and Installing the Factory Default Configuration 14
    Hands-On Exercise 1.4.2: Using ASDM to Build an Initial Configuration on Your ASA 5505 15
    Hands-On Exercise 1.4.2: Previewing Commands 18
Hands-On Exercise 2.1: Analyzing the Base Configuration and Saving It 18
    Hands-On Exercise 2.1.1: Confirm Network Connectivity 19
    Hands-On Exercise 2.1.2: Review and Backup Configuration Information 19
Hands-On Exercise 2.2: Backing Up and Restoring the Configuration 21
    Hands-On Exercise 2.2.1: Install and Configure the TFTP Server Software on Your PC 21
    Hands-On Exercise 2.2.2: The Backup Process 21
    Hands-On Exercise 2.2.3: The Restore Process 21
Hands-On Exercise 2.3: Backing Up and Restoring the Software Image 22
    Hands-On Exercise 2.3.1: Backup Your ASA 5505's Software to the TFTP Server 22
    Hands-On Exercise 2.3.2: Restore the ASA Software in ROM Monitor 23
Hands-On Exercise 3.1: Sending Logging Output to a Syslog Server 24
    Enable Remote Logging 24
    Test the Logging Configuration 24
Hands-On Exercise 4.1: Telnet and Secure Shell (SSH) 25
    Hands-On Exercise 4.1.1: Configuring and Using Telnet 25
        Disconnecting Telnet Sessions 26

Copyright 2016, soundtraining.net. All rights reserved. It is illegal to make copies of this document in any form. www.soundtraining.net If you believe this is an illegal copy, please contact soundtraining.net at (206) 988-5858.

Hands-On Exercise 4.1.2: Configuring and Using SSH (Secure Shell) 26
  Test the SSH Configuration 27
  Disconnecting SSH Sessions 27
Hands-On Exercise 5.1: Creating Banners on the Security Appliance 28
  Test the Banner Configuration 28
Hands-On Exercise 5.2: Configuring Usernames and Local Authentication 28
  Building the Configuration in the ASDM 29
  Testing the Configuration 30
Hands-On Exercise 5.3: Configuring ASA Authentication through Active Directory 31
  Prerequisites 31
  Configuration Steps 31
Hands-On Exercise 6.1: Reconfiguring Your DHCP Server 32
  Assign a Different IP Address to Your Inside Interface 32
  Configure a New DHCP Pool 33
Hands-On Exercise 8.1: Site-to-Site VPNs 34
  Hands-On Exercise 8.1.1: Save the Appliance's Current Running Configuration to Flash Memory 34
  Hands-On Exercise 8.1.2: Attempt the Remote Connection 34
    Building the Tunnel 35
    Create the Network Objects 35
    Create an Access-Control List 36
    Create and Configure the Tunnel Group 36
    Configure Phase 1 36
    Configure Phase 2 37
    Configure NAT 37
    Configure a Default Route 37
  Hands-On Exercise 8.1.3: Wrapping up the Site-to-Site VPN Exercise 38
Hands-On Exercise 8.2: Configuring a Cisco AnyConnect Remote Access VPN 38
  Hands-On Exercise 8.2.1: Building the Basic AnyConnect Configuration 38
    Prerequisite 38
    Configuration Steps 39
  Hands-On Exercise 8.2.2: Configuring ASA VPN Authentication through Active Directory Using RADIUS 40
  Prerequisites 40
  Configuration Steps 41

Copyright 2016, soundtraining.net. All rights reserved. It is illegal to make copies of this document in any form. www.soundtraining.net If you believe this is an illegal copy, please contact soundtraining.net at (206) 988-5858.

- Sample Configuration 41
- Hands-On Exercise 8.2.3: Configuring Kerberos Authentication 42
- Hands-On Exercise 8.2.4: Configuring LDAP Authentication 42
- Hands-On Exercise 9.1: Configuring a DMZ 42
  - Installing the Abyss Web Server Software 49
    - Allowing Inside Hosts and Internet Hosts Access to the DMZ Web Server 50
- Hands-On Exercise 9.2: Analyzing Potential Vulnerabilities with Port Scanning 51
- Hands-On Exercise 10.1: Filtering Dynamic Content 52
- Hands-On Exercise 11.1: Viewing and Changing the Mode 53
- Support and Online Resources 55
  - Technical Support 55
  - Online Support 55
- Building Your IT Career 55
- Books for IT Pros 55
- Errors 55

Copyright 2016, soundtraining.net. All rights reserved. It is illegal to make copies of this document in any form. www.soundtraining.net If you believe this is an illegal copy, please contact soundtraining.net at (206) 988-5858.

Prerequisites for Successfully Using this Lab Manual

The lab exercises in this manual require the following:

A server at 192.168.0.1 configured as follows (I use a Windows Active Directory Domain Controller for simplicity, but this could certainly be done with a UNIX or Linux server.):

- RADIUS (Watch my video at https://youtu.be/1yYywwPWXys to learn how to build this server.)
- LDAP configured with dc=soundtraining and dc=local
- Kerberos with a Kerberos realm of soundtraining.local
- Web server, including a directory titled applets. I downloaded several Java applets from www.realapplets.com for use in exercise 10.1.
- FTP server
- DNS configured as follows:
    - A or CNAME record mapping www.soundtraining.local to 192.168.0.1
    - A or CNAME record mapping ftp.soundtraining.local to 192.168.0.1
- DHCP configured as follows:
    - Pool: 192.168.0.0/24
    - Gateway: 192.168.0.1
    - DNS: 192.168.0.1

Student workstations including the following software:

- PuTTY (You can also use TeraTerm or any other terminal emulation software.)
- tftpd32, tftpd64, or some other TFTP server software.
- Abyss Web server
- nmap

General Instructions for the Student

- Instructions are written in Times New Roman.
- `Console output from the ASA is written in Courier New`
- **`Commands to be executed are written in Courier New Bold.`**
- Output and commands follow the generic prompt `ciscoasa#`. Your actual prompt may be different. For example, your prompt may be the hostname of your device. Do not type the prompt.
- Read all instructions thoroughly before starting the exercise.
- Check off each instruction as you complete it.
- Please do not work ahead.
- Please ask questions for clarification.
- The classroom web server and FTP server are located at 192.168.0.1.
- Please ask for help at any time. Learning is supposed to be fun. If you find yourself getting frustrated, ask for help!
- Like all software vendors, Cisco makes frequent changes to their software. If a command does not work the way you expect it to, check to ensure you're using the same software version as this document. This workbook is based on ASA software versions 9.11 and 9.14 and ASDM version 7.3(1).

Copyright 2016, soundtraining.net. All rights reserved. It is illegal to make copies of this document in any form. www.soundtraining.net If you believe this is an illegal copy, please contact soundtraining.net at (206) 988-5858.

Hands-On Exercise 1.1: Password Recovery and Initial Configuration

In this exercise, you will begin the process of configuring your firewall from scratch. You will use password recovery procedures to reset the password to a known value, you will record important information about the firewall, and you will then erase the configuration and build a new configuration from scratch.

Hands-On Exercise 1.1.1: Connecting to the Security Appliance's Console Port

1. Open PuTTY on your PC (Alternatively, you may use any terminal emulation software you wish such as HyperTerminal, TeraTerm, or others.): Click on Start, then click on All Programs>>PuTTY. Click on the PuTTY application to start the PuTTY application.
2. Configure PuTTY with the following settings:
Connection type: Serial
Click "Open"

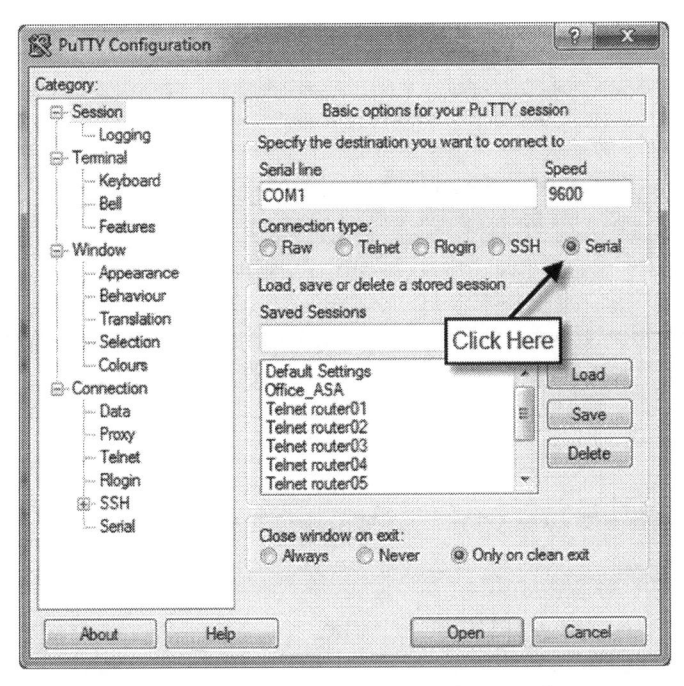

(It is not necessary to configure the following settings manually in PuTTY. They are included here as a reference in case you are using a different terminal program: Connect using: COM1, Bits per second: 9600, Data bits: 8, Parity: None, Stop bits: 1, Flow control: None)

Hands-On Exercise 1.1.2: Password Recovery on the Security Appliance

This procedure will require you to power-cycle your appliance by unplugging it at the power strip and plugging it back in. You will then interrupt the boot process and change the configuration register to prevent the appliance from reading its stored configuration at boot.

1. Power-cycle your appliance by removing and re-inserting the plug at the power strip.
2. When prompted, press Esc to interrupt the boot process and enter ROM Monitor mode. You should immediately see a rommon prompt (`rommon #0>`).

3. At the rommon prompt, enter the confreg command to view the current configuration register setting:
   `rommon #0>`**`confreg`**
4. The current configuration register should be the default of 0x01 (it will actually display as 0x00000001). The security appliance will ask if you want to make changes to the configuration register. Answer no when prompted.
5. You must change the configuration register to 0x41, which tells the appliance to ignore its saved (startup) configuration upon boot:
   `rommon #1>`**`confreg 0x41`**
6. Reset the appliance with the boot command:
   `rommon #2>`**`boot`**
7. Notice that the security appliance ignores its startup configuration during the boot process. When it finishes booting, you should see a generic User Mode prompt:
   `ciscoasa>`
8. Enter the enable command to enter Privileged Mode. When the appliance prompts you for a password, simply press <Enter> (at this point, the password is blank):
   `ciscoasa>`**`enable`**
   `Password:<Enter>`
   `ciscoasa#`
9. Copy the startup configuration file into the running configuration with the following command:
   `ciscoasa#`**`copy startup-config running-config`**
   Destination filename [running-config]?<Enter>
10. The previously saved configuration is now the active configuration, but since the security appliance is already in Privileged Mode, privileged access is not disabled. Next, in configuration mode, enter the following command to change the Privileged Mode password to a known value (in this case, we'll use the password p@ss5678):
    `ciscoasa#`**`conf t`**
    `ciscoasa(config)#`**`enable password p@ss5678`**
11. Your security appliance may also be configured to support user authentication. You can check it to determine if user authentication is enabled with the following command:
    `ciscoasa#`**`show run aaa`**
12. If you see output similar to this, user authentication has been enabled (note: Not all firewalls will be configured for aaa authentication. Neither will all firewalls display all of the following configuration lines):
    `ciscoasa#`**`show run aaa`**
    `aaa authentication enable console LOCAL`
    `aaa authentication serial console LOCAL`
    `aaa authentication ssh console LOCAL`
    `aaa authorization command LOCAL`
13. In the above output, local user database authentication has been enabled for privileged mode console logons (enable), serial console logons, ssh console logons, and for various levels of commands. In a "real-world" situation, you may or may not want to disable such authentication, but if you do not know the passwords required to access the security appliance, you will have to disable aaa authentication with the following configuration mode commands (and for the purpose of this exercise, please execute the following commands):

```
ciscoasa(config)#no aaa authentication enable console LOCAL
ciscoasa(config)#no aaa authentication serial console LOCAL
ciscoasa(config)#no aaa authentication ssh console LOCAL
ciscoasa(config)#no aaa authorization command LOCAL
```
14. While still in Configuration Mode, reset the configuration register to the default of 0x01 to force the security appliance to read its startup configuration on boot:
```
ciscoasa(config)#config-register 0x01
```
15. Use the following commands to view the configuration register setting:
```
ciscoasa(config)#exit
ciscoasa#show version
```
16. At bottom of the output of the show version command, you should see the following statement:
```
Configuration register is 0x41 (will be 0x1 at next reload)
```
17. Save the current configuration with the copy run start command to make the above changes persistent:
```
ciscoasa#copy run start
Source filename [running-config] <Enter>
```
18. Reload the security appliance:
```
ciscoasa# reload
System config has been modified. Save? [Y]es/[N]o:yes
Cryptochecksum: e87f1433 54896e6b 4e21d072 d71a9cbf
2149 bytes copied in 1.480 secs (2149 bytes/sec)
Proceed with reload? [confirm]<Enter>
```

For Your Information: Disallowing Password Recovery

It is possible to prevent password recovery. In configuration mode, use the command "**no service password-recovery**". When that command is enabled, the user is prevented from entering ROMMON mode with the configuration intact. When a user attempts to enter ROMMON mode for password recovery, the ASA prompts the user to erase all flash file systems. They cannot enter ROMMON mode without doing that, which would make the ASA non-functional until a new software image is loaded and the configuration is rebuilt or restored from backup.

Hands-On Exercise 1.2: Removing the Existing Configuration

In this exercise, you will return your ASA 5505 to a blank configuration.

1. Log in to the console port on your ASA and enter privileged mode:
   ```
   ciscoasa> en
   Password: p@ss5678
   ciscoasa#
   ```
2. Enter configuration mode:
   ```
   ciscoasa# config t
   ciscoasa(config)#
   ```
3. Enter the following commands to reset your ASA 5505 to a blank configuration:
   ```
   ciscoasa(config)# write erase
   Erase configuration in flash memory? [confirm]<Enter>
   ciscoasa(config)# reload
   Proceed with reload? [confirm]<Enter>
   ```

When your ASA 5505 finishes reloading, it will ask if you want to pre-configure the firewall through interactive prompts. Type **no** and press the Enter key.

Hands-On Exercise 1.3: Using the Eight Commands Required to Enable Basic Firewall Functionality

In this exercise, you will use the command-line interface to build a basic firewall configuration that will allow local traffic out, but not allow external traffic in.

Assign Interface Names, IP Addresses, and a Default Route

1. Log in with a blank username and password.
   ```
   ciscoasa> en
   Password: <Enter>
   ```
2. Identify the logical (VLAN) interfaces, assign names and security levels to them:
   ```
   ciscoasa# conf t
   ```
   (The ASA will now ask if you wish to enable anonymous reporting. Enter **N** for no.)
   ```
   ciscoasa(config)# interface vlan1
   ciscoasa(config-if)# nameif inside
   INFO: Security level for "inside" set to 100 by default.
   ciscoasa(config-if)# interface vlan2
   ciscoasa(config-if)# nameif outside
   INFO: Security level for "outside" set to 0 by default.
   ```
3. Assign physical interfaces to each of the logical interfaces and enable the physical interfaces:
   ```
   ciscoasa(config-if)# interface ethernet 0/0
   ciscoasa(config-if)# switchport access vlan 2
   ciscoasa(config-if)# no shutdown
   ciscoasa(config-if)# interface ethernet 0/1
   ciscoasa(config-if)# switchport access vlan 1
   ciscoasa(config-if)# no shutdown
   ```

Copyright 2016, soundtraining.net. All rights reserved. It is illegal to make copies of this document in any form. www.soundtraining.net If you believe this is an illegal copy, please contact soundtraining.net at (206) 988-5858.

4. Assign IP addresses to the logical interfaces. Use a static address on the inside interface and a DHCP assigned address on the outside interface:
   ```
   ciscoasa(config-if)# interface vlan 2
   ciscoasa(config-if)# ip address dhcp
   ciscoasa(config-if)# interface vlan 1
   ciscoasa(config-if)# ip address 192.168.1.1
   ```
5. Configure a default route:
   ```
   ciscoasa(config-if)# route outside 0 0 192.168.0.1
   ```
   (Note: 192.168.0.1 is a gateway address often used on private local area networks. If you are configuring an ASA connected to the public Internet, you will obtain the gateway address from your service provider. It is strongly recommended that, during the learning process on the ASA, you not be connected directly to the public Internet.)

Configure Port Address Translation

6. Create a network object group to identify the IP addresses of hosts permitted to use PAT. In this example, it will be all hosts. (**Note: the last command in this step spans two lines in this documentation, but should be entered on a single line in the ASA command-line.**):
   ```
   ciscoasa# conf t
   ciscoasa(config)# object network obj_any
   ciscoasa(config-network-object)# subnet 0.0.0.0 0.0.0.0
   ciscoasa(config-network-object)# nat (inside,outside) dynamic interface
   ```

Test the Configuration

7. Assign a static IP address to your management workstation to test your configuration (the following steps are for computers running the Windows 7 operating system):
   a. Click on *Start*, then click on *Control Panel*
   b. Click on *Network and Internet Connections*
   c. Click on *Network and Sharing Center*
   d. Click on *Change Adapter Settings*
   e. Right-click on *Local Area Connection* for the wired connection and select *Properties*
   f. Scroll down to and double-click on *Internet Protocol Version 4 (TCP/IPv4)* to display its properties sheet
   g. Select the radio button labeled Use the following IP address and enter the following parameters:
      i. IP address: 192.168.1.2
      ii. Subnet mask: 255.255.255.0
      iii. Default gateway: 192.168.1.1
      iv. DNS server: 192.168.0.1 (you need to enter only one DNS server for this exercise)
   h. Click OK as needed to save the configuration and exit the applet.
8. Test your configuration by attempting to connect to the classroom website from your PC at http://www.soundtraining.local or 192.168.0.1

9. When you have successfully connected to the website, restore your computer's IP configuration to obtain an IP address automatically.

Hands-On Exercise 1.4: Building a Base Configuration on the ASA Security Appliance

In this exercise, you will once again return your ASA 5505 to the basic factory default configuration. This time, however, instead of building the configuration from scratch in the Command-Line Interface, you will use the Adaptive Security Device Manager to build the configuration.

Hands-On Exercise 1.4.1: Removing the Existing Configuration on Your Security Appliance and Installing the Factory Default Configuration

1. Log in to the console port on your ASA and enter privileged mode:
   ```
   ciscoasa> en
   Password: <Enter>
   ciscoasa#
   ```
2. Enter configuration mode:
   ```
   ciscoasa# config t
   ciscoasa(config)#
   ```
3. Enter the following commands to reset your ASA 5505 to factory defaults (if your appliance asks to save the configuration, say "no"):
   ```
   ciscoasa(config)# write erase
   Erase configuration in flash memory? [confirm]<Enter>
   ciscoasa(config)# reload
   Proceed with reload? [confirm]<Enter>
   ```
   (If your security appliance asks if you want to save the modified configuration, say "no".)
4. When your ASA 5505 finishes reloading, it will ask if you want to pre-configure the firewall through interactive prompts. Type no and press the Enter key.
5. Set your ASA 5505 to its factory default configuration with the following commands (in configuration mode):
   ```
   ciscoasa> enable
   Password: <Enter>
   ciscoasa#
   ciscoasa# config t
   ```
   (Again, the ASA will ask if you wish to enable anonymous reporting. Enter *N* for no.)
   ```
   ciscoasa(config)# config factory-default
   ```
   (Press the space bar at each "-more-" prompt.
6. Reset your management workstation to obtain an IP address automatically:
   a. Click on *Start*, then click on *Control Panel*
   b. Click on *Network and Internet Connections*
   c. Click on *Network Connections*
   d. Right-click on *Local Area Connection* and select *Properties*
   e. Scroll down to and double-click on *Internet Protocol (TCP/IP)* to display its properties sheet
   f. Select the radio button labeled *Obtain an IP address automatically*.

g. Click OK as needed to save the configuration and exit the applet.
h. Confirm that your PC obtained an IP address by clicking *Start*, then *Run*. (Alternatively, you can use the key combination of Win+R.) In the Run dialog box, type *cmd* and press the Enter key.
i. In the Command Line Interface window that appears, type *ipconfig* and press the Enter key.
j. You should see an IP address of 192.168.1.5 (or possibly a different number in the fourth position) with a subnet mask of 255.255.255.0 and a default gateway of 192.168.1.1. If you do not see these values, type the command *ipconfig /renew* in the Command Line Interface window and press the Enter key. You should now see an IP address of 192.168.1.5 (or possibly a slightly different number in the fourth position) with a subnet mask of 255.255.255.0 and a default gateway of 192.168.1.1. If you do not see these values, review the preceding steps and, if necessary, repeat them.

Hands-On Exercise 1.4.2: Using ASDM to Build an Initial Configuration on Your ASA 5505

In this portion of the exercise, you will use the Adaptive Security Device Manager to build an initial (basic) configuration on your security appliance. This configuration will be the basis for all subsequent exercises.

From your PC, use the browser to connect to the ASA 5505:

1. On your PC, click Start>Run (or use the key combination of Win+R)
2. Enter the following URL in the Run dialog window:
   https://192.168.1.1
   (note the use of the "s" in the protocol type)
3. For the purpose of this exercise, ignore the certificate warning and proceed to the website. (Obviously, in a "real-world" environment, you would use standard security precautions before proceeding.)
4. If you get an ActiveX/Java warning in your browser, run the add-in.
5. After several seconds, the Cisco ASDM 7.1(2) page should appear. If it appears, go to step 7. If, instead, you see a pop-up error saying "Unable to launch device manager" or "Application Blocked by Java Security", you probably need to adjust the Java security settings on your computer.
6. To deal with this error, go to Control Panel >> Java. Select the Security tab and add the IP address of the ASA to the Java Exception Site List. (When you add the ASA's IP

address, you must also include https://.)

7. If a button is visible in the lower right-hand corner of the screen labeled *Run Startup Wizard*, proceed to step 11. Otherwise, proceed to step 8.

8. If a button is visible at the bottom of the screen prompting you to install Java, you must install the Java runtime environment. Simply click it to install Java. This requires an Internet connection or it can downloaded from the classroom Web server.

9. Java will take some time to install and may appear to stall. It will, however, eventually complete the installation.

10. When Java Runtime is completed, you can continue the exercise by refreshing your browser.

11. Click the button in the lower right-hand corner of the screen labeled *Run Startup Wizard*. You will receive several security warnings and additional requests for authentication. Click Yes or OK on all subsequent security warnings and authentication requests (leaving username and password fields blank).

12. If a Windows security alert appears, click the button labeled "*Unblock*" or "*Allow*".

13. A Cisco Smart Call Home window will appear (on some software versions, you will not see this). Select the radio button labeled *Do not enable Smart Call Home* and press OK.

14. Press OK again to confirm that you do not want to enable Smart Call Home.

15. The *Startup Wizard: Starting Point* window will appear. Ensure that the radio button for *Modify existing configuration* is selected and click the button at the bottom of the window labeled Next.

Copyright 2016, soundtraining.net. All rights reserved. It is illegal to make copies of this document in any form. www.soundtraining.net If you believe this is an illegal copy, please contact soundtraining.net at (206) 988-5858.

16. The *Startup Wizard: Basic Configuration* window will appear.
17. Enter the *ASA Host Name* for your security appliance (this is the name on the label on your security appliance).
18. Enter *soundtraining.local* for the domain name.
19. Check the box labeled *Change the privileged mode (enable) password.* Leave the Old Password field blank and enter *p@ss5678* for the New Password and confirm it.
20. Click the button labeled *Next*.
21. The *Interface Selection* window appears. Configure the settings on this page as follows:
    a. Outside VLAN: Leave the default settings in place (VLAN 2, enable VLAN)
    b. Inside VLAN: Leave the default settings in place (VLAN 1, enable VLAN)
    c. Newer versions of ASDM do not include a DMZ option, but if you see an option for DMZ VLAN: Choose *Do not configure* and clear the check box labeled Enable VLAN.
22. Click the button labeled *Next >*.
23. The *Switch Port Allocation* page appears. Although it is not necessary to make any changes on this page, notice that ports Ethernet 0/1 through Ethernet 0/7 are allocated to VLAN 1 (the inside VLAN) and port Ethernet 0/0 is allocated to VLAN 2 (the outside VLAN). Click the button labeled *Next >*.
24. The *Interface IP Address Configuration* page appears.
    a. In the *Outside IP Address* section, choose the default setting to use DHCP.)
    b. In the *Inside IP Address* section, leave the default settings in place (192.168.1.1 and 255.255.255.0).
25. Click the button labeled *Next >*.
26. The *DHCP Server* page appears.
27. Ensure that the checkbox to *Enable DHCP server on the inside interface* is selected.
28. In the *DHCP Address Pool* section, accept the default starting and ending IP addresses (this is based on the licensed number of users).
29. In the *DHCP Parameters* section, enter the following parameters:
    a. DNS Server 1: 192.168.0.1
    b. DNS Server 2: blank
    c. WINS Server 1: blank
    d. WINS Server 2: blank
    e. Lease Length: 86400 secs (default is 3600 seconds; 86400 secs is one day)
    f. Ping Timeout: 50 ms (default is 50 ms)
    g. Domain name: soundtraining.local

30. Click the button labeled *Next >*.

31. The *Address Translation (NAT/PAT)* page appears. Select the radio button labeled *Use Port Address Translation (PAT)* and ensure that the button labeled *Use the IP address on the outside interface* is selected.

32. Click the button labeled *Next >*.

33. The *Administrative Access* page appears. The default settings allow access from the 192.168.1.0 network (which is what has enabled you to run the ASDM up to this point). It is not necessary to make any changes. (You could also enable SSH and Telnet access on this page, but you will do that manually later in the workshop.)

34. Click the button labeled *Next >*.

35. The *Startup Wizard Summary* page appears. Review the settings to ensure they're what you expect. When you are satisfied, click the button labeled *Finish*.

36. The ASDM will sometimes hang at 11-17%. If that happens, click the red "X" in the upper right-hand corner of the "Please wait..." window. In the next dialog box, click *Continue*.

37. The device will prompt you for a username and password. Leave the username field blank and enter *p@ss5678* for the password.

38. You are now logged in to the Adaptive Security Device Manager.

> **Note:** After building the configuration, the ASDM may ask you if you want to enable *Smart Call Home*. This is a feature which was introduced into the ASA firewalls in version 8.2. *Smart Call Home* allows for periodic monitoring of the firewall device. It provides real-time troubleshooting information to the Cisco Technical Assistance Center. *Smart Call Home* is included in a Cisco SmartNET contract. For the purpose of this exercise, do not enable *Smart Call Home*. For more information about its capabilities, see the video at
> http://www.cisco.com/warp/public/437/services/smartcallhome/

Hands-On Exercise 1.4.2: Previewing Commands

Configure the ASDM to allow you to preview the commands you enable before sending them to the device with the following commands:

1. In the menu bar at the top of the ASDM window, click on *Tools*, then click on *Preferences...*

2. In the *Preferences* window, under the *General* tab, check the box to *Preview commands before sending them to the device.* and click *OK*.

Hands-On Exercise 2.1: Analyzing the Base Configuration and Saving It

It is a good idea to record important information about your ASA for future reference including the license information and activation key. In this exercise, you will review your appliance's hardware and software configuration including license, serial number, and activation key and create a text file backup of the information.

Hands-On Exercise 2.1.1: Confirm Network Connectivity

In its default configuration, the ASA 5505 will provide DHCP services. Test the DHCP service on your PC with the following commands:

1. Click Start>Run (or use the key combination of Win+R)
2. Type **cmd**
3. In the command prompt window, enter `ipconfig /renew`.
4. After a few seconds, you should see IP address parameters similar to this:

   ```
   Ethernet adapter Local Area Connection:

           Connection-specific DNS Suffix  . :
           IP Address. . . . . . . . . . . . : 192.168.1.2
           Subnet Mask . . . . . . . . . . . : 255.255.255.0
           Default Gateway . . . . . . . . . : 192.168.1.1
   ```

   If your settings are substantially different from this, review the preceding steps and make corrections as needed.

5. Confirm connectivity by pinging your ASA's inside interface from your PC, using the following command:
   `C:\>ping 192.168.1.1`

Hands-On Exercise 2.1.2: Review and Backup Configuration Information

1. Create a folder on your management workstation to store all of your configuration files: On your management workstation, create a folder called c:\myconfigs (alternatively, you could create a folder on a flash drive to store all of your configuration files). If you're not familiar with how to create a new folder, ask your instructor for assistance.

2. Using PuTTY to connect to your computer's serial port, in your ASA's command-line interface (CLI), enter the following commands:

   ```
   ciscoasa> enable
   Password:<Enter>
   ciscoasa# terminal pager 0
   ```
   (Terminal pager determines how many lines of text will be shown on your monitor in a single page. Setting terminal pager to 0 disables paging.)

3. To open the PuTTY configuration menu, click on the small PuTTY icon in the upper left-hand corner of the PuTTY window.

4. Click on the menu option *Change Settings..*

5. In the PuTTY Reconfiguration window, in the category tree on the left, under *Session*, click on *Logging*.

6. On the right-hand side of the *Reconfiguration* window, under *Session logging*, click the radio button labeled *Printable output*.

7. In the Log file name field, browse to *c:\myconfigs*. Name the file asainfo.txt and click *Save*.

8. Click *Apply*.

9. In your ASA 5505's console window, enter the following command:

   `ciscoasa# `**`show version`**

10. When the output finishes displaying, restore the paging of command-line output with the following command:

    `ciscoasa# `**`terminal pager 24`**

11. Click again on the PuTTY icon in the upper right-hand corner of the PuTTY window, click again on *Change Settings…*

12. On the right-hand side of the PuTTY *Reconfiguration* window, under *Session logging*, click the radio button labeled *None* to disable logging.

13. Click *Apply*.

14. Find the folder *c:\myconfigs* (or whatever folder you created to store your configuration files), then find the file asainfo.txt. Right-click on it with your mouse, choose "*Open with Wordpad*" to view the contents. (I recommend Wordpad instead of Notepad because Wordpad formats the text to make it easier to read.)

15. What is the system image file and where is it stored?
    (The system image file will have a name similar to asa911-k8.bin and should be located in flash, also known as disk0.)

16. What type of CPU does the ASA 5505 use?
    (ASA 5505 appliances use a Geode processor which is often found in purpose-built devices such as the ASA.)

17. How much RAM is available on the ASA?

18. How much Flash Memory is available on the ASA?

19. How many physical interfaces are supported on this ASA?
    (You should find eight physical interfaces on the ASA 5505.)

20. How many VLANs does this ASA support?
    (The number of supported VLANs will vary based on the license. A 5505 with a base license supports three VLANs, but one of them is restricted.)

21. How many inside hosts are supported with this license?
    (This number varies based on the license.)

22. How many VPN peers are supported with this license?   SSL VPN clients?
    (As with the number of inside hosts, this number also varies based on the license.)

23. What type of license is associated with this ASA?

24. What is the serial number of this ASA?
    (The serial number is important to note when you need to obtain service from Cisco and when you want to upgrade your device's license.)

25. Notice the activation key. The activation key is tied to your device's serial number and determines the features that are enabled on your device.

26. What is the configuration register for this ASA?
    (The configuration register is a 16-bit software value that tells the device how to boot. For example, in a previous exercise, you modified the configuration register to 0x41 which told the device to ignore its saved configuration, thus allowing you to perform password recovery procedures on the device.)

Hands-On Exercise 2.2: Backing Up and Restoring the Configuration

Now that you have built a base configuration on your firewall, you will want to create a backup to facilitate disaster recovery. In this exercise, you will backup and restore your security appliance's running configuration to and from a TFTP server.

Hands-On Exercise 2.2.1: Install and Configure the TFTP Server Software on Your PC

1. On your PC, navigate to www.soundtraining.local and download tftpd32 or tftpd64.
2. After you downloaded the TFTP server, install it on your management workstation.
3. When the installation completes, click on Start>All Programs and find tftpd32. Start it.
4. In the TFTP server application window, notice that the current directory is c:\Program Files (x86)\tftpd32 or something similar.
5. Change the TFTP root folder to c:\myconfigs (or whatever folder you created earlier to store your configurations).

It may also be necessary to configure the Windows firewall to allow incoming TFTP connections by clicking the button labeled Unblock, if prompted.

Hands-On Exercise 2.2.2: The Backup Process

In your security appliance's CLI, execute the following commands to backup your running configuration to a TFTP server.

1. ```
   ciscoasa> enable <Enter>
   ciscoasa# copy running-config tftp://192.168.1.5 <Enter>
   ```
   (where 192.168.1.5 is the address of your management workstation. If yours' is different, make necessary adjustments.)
   ```
   Source filename [running-config]? <Enter>
   Address or name of remote host [192.168.1.5]? <Enter>
   ```
   (where 192.168.1.5 is the IP address of your management workstation)
   ```
   Destination filename [running-config]? asa_backup.txt
   <Enter>
   ```
2. You will see a confirmation of the transfer in the appliance's console output.
3. Confirm the transfer by checking for the file in the TFTP root folder.

Hands-On Exercise 2.2.3: The Restore Process

Rename your security appliance with the following commands:
   ```

1. ```
   ciscoasa# config t <enter>
   ciscoasa(config)# hostname asatest <enter>
   asatest(config)# exit <enter>
   asatest#
   ```
   Notice that the security appliance's prompt has changed to reflect the new hostname. You will now copy the previously backed up configuration from the TFTP server to the security appliance's running configuration with the following commands:
2. ```
   asatest# copy tftp://192.168.1.5/asa_backup.txt running-config <Enter>
   ```
   (192.168.1.5 is the IP address of your management workstation. If yours' is different, you must adjust settings or commands accordingly.)
3. `Address or name of remote host [192.168.1.5]?<Enter>`
   (where 192.168.1.5 is the address of your management workstation)
4. `Source filename [asa_backup.txt]? <enter>`
5. `Destination filename [running-config]?<Enter>`

You will notice confirmation of the transfer, plus some error messages related to duplicate NAT entries. When the transfer is completed, notice that your security appliance's prompt reflects the original hostname.

Hands-On Exercise 2.3: Backing Up and Restoring the Software Image

In this series of exercises, you will create backups of your ASA's software using a TFTP server. You will then copy the ASA software from your TFTP server into the ASA 5505's flash memory using the same techniques you would use to restore a backup of the software or to perform an upgrade.

Hands-On Exercise 2.3.1: Backup Your ASA 5505's Software to the TFTP Server

Ensure that the TFTP server is running on your management workstation.

1. Display the contents of your security appliance's flash memory:
   `ciscoasa# show flash <enter>`
   Notice a file named similarly to *asa911-k8.bin*. That is the security appliance's software image (similar to a computer's operating system).

2. Copy the software image to your TFTP server with the following commands:

   ```
   ciscoasa# copy flash tftp <enter>
   Source filename []:asa911-k8.bin <enter>
   ```

   (Note: If your security appliance is running a different version of the software, you will have to adjust these commands to reflect the correct version numbers.)

   `Address or name of remote host []? 192.168.1.5 <enter>`

   (where 192.168.1.5 is the address of your management workstation)

   `Destination filename [asa911-k8.bin]? <Enter>`

3. Your security appliance console output will display many lines of exclamation marks as it copies the software to the TFTP server. This process can take several minutes. You can watch the progress in the TFTP server console window. (This is also a good time to take a short break.)

Note: In a real-world setting, you will probably want to backup the ASDM image as well. It has a filename similar to asdm-712.bin.

Hands-On Exercise 2.3.2: Restore the ASA Software in ROM Monitor

1. Enter the following command to reload your security appliance:
   ciscoasa# **reload**
   System config has been modified. Save? [Y]es/[N]o: (choose Y to save any changes you made)
   Proceed with reload?[confirm] <Enter>
2. When you see the prompt to use BREAK or ESC to interrupt boot, press *Esc* to interrupt the boot process and enter rommon (ROM Monitor Mode).
3. In rommon, enter the following commands (note that the actual rommon prompt will include a line number, for example rommon #3):

   rommon> **interface ethernet 0/1** <Enter>

   MAC Address: XXXX.XXXX.XXXX

   Link is UP

   rommon> **address 192.168.1.1** <Enter>

   rommon> **server 192.168.1.2** <Enter>

   rommon> **file asa911-k8.bin** <Enter>
4. **Important:** Review the previous configuration to ensure that all information has been entered correctly and that the IP addresses listed in this document correspond to the actual IP addresses in use on your LAN segment. (If you happen to make a mistake, the security appliance will make 20 attempts to connect to the TFTP server before it times out.)
5. On your management workstation, use the ipconfig command to view its IP address. Notice that it no longer has an address on the 192.168.1.0 network and instead displays an address on the 169.254.0.0 network. This is due to your security appliance operating in ROM Monitor mode which does not support DHCP services. Manually assign the static IP address of 192.168.1.2 to your management workstation with a subnet mask of 255.255.255.0. If you are uncertain about how to do this, ask your instructor for assistance. It is not necessary to assign a default gateway nor any other IP parameters.
6. When you are satisfied that everything is correct, initiate the file transfer with the following command:
   rommon> **tftp** <Enter>
   (This procedure is considerably faster than backing up the software.)
7. Depending on your firewall's software version, you may have to enter the following command to boot your security appliance normally:
   rommon> **boot** <Enter>

8. Reset your management workstation to obtain an IP address automatically. If you're not sure how to do this, ask you instructor for assistance.
9. You should see an IP address of 192.168.1.5 with a subnet mask of 255.255.255.0 and a default gateway of 192.168.1.1. If you do not see these values, type the command ipconfig /renew in the Command Line Interface window and press the Enter key. You should now see an IP address of 192.168.1.5 with a subnet mask of 255.255.255.0 and a default gateway of 192.168.1.1.
10. Confirm that the software was copied into the appliance's flash with the show flash command. (In the real world, if you had to do this, there would be size differences between the new and old files. In this exercise, you shouldn't be able to tell any difference.)

Hands-On Exercise 3.1: Sending Logging Output to a Syslog Server

In this exercise, you will configure and enable logging from your ASA security appliance to a syslog server.

The tftpd32 (or tftpd64) software you installed earlier includes a syslog server, which is based on the UNIX syslogd daemon, a centralized logging server.

Enable Remote Logging

Enable remote logging on your security appliance with the following commands in *global configuration mode*.

1. Identify the syslog server:
   ciscoasa(config)# **logging host inside 192.168.1.5** <enter>
   (where 192.168.1.5 represents the IP address of your management workstation)

2. Configure the level of logging:
   ciscoasa(config)# **logging trap informational** <enter>
   (This is a fairly heavy level of logging which is appropriate for testing use, but would probably be too heavy for routine production use.)

3. Add timestamps to the logging entries:
   ciscoasa(config)# **logging timestamp** <enter>
   (syslog will include a timestamp based on the logging host time. You might, however, want to have the security appliance timestamp log entries based on the appliance' time.)

4. Tell the ASA to identify itself by its hostname in the logging entries:
   ciscoasa(config)# **logging device-id hostname** <enter>

5. Enable logging:
   ciscoasa(config)# **logging enable** <enter>

Test the Logging Configuration

1. In order for your firewall to know what to do with the ping command in the next step, you must also configure a default route with the following command:
   ciscoasa(config)# **route outside 0 0 192.168.0.1** <enter>

(where "0 0" represents any network and any mask and 192.168.0.1 is the IP address of the default gateway).

2. Execute a ping to a non-existent address:
   `ciscoasa(config)# ping 4.1.1.1 <enter>`
3. Notice that Syslog records the attempted ping.
4. Change the logging level to warning and notice how much quieter syslog becomes:
   `ciscoasa(config)# logging trap warning <enter>`

You may need to expand the column labeled *text* in order to see the logging information.

Now that you have made additional changes to your configuration, save it to flash memory and back it up to your TFTP server using the procedures you learned earlier. (Hint: You can use the simple command `wr` to write the configuration to flash memory. It is the same as `copy running-config startup-config`.)

`ciscoasa# wr`

`ciscoasa# copy run tftp://192.168.1.5/config_syslog.txt <enter>`
(where 192.168.1.5 is the IP address of your TFTP server)

Note: As you have probably noticed, tftpd32 (tftpd64) is a very basic syslog server with limited features. There are commercial products such as KiwiSyslog offering a much more extensive feature set. Configuration of the ASA is the same, regardless of your choice of syslog server.

Hands-On Exercise 4.1: Telnet and Secure Shell (SSH)

Hands-On Exercise 4.1.1: Configuring and Using Telnet

Telnet is a legacy, non-secure protocol and should only be used if SSH is unavailable. For that reason, Telnet cannot be used on the outside interface of the security appliance, except through a VPN tunnel.

These steps must be done in a console session via your serial console cable.

1. Begin by configuring the address(es) from which the Adaptive Security Appliance will accept connections:
   ```
   ciscoasa> en <enter>
   Password: p@ss5678 <enter>
   ciscoasa# config t <enter>
   ciscoasa(config)# telnet 192.168.1.0 255.255.255.0 inside <enter>
   ```
   (where "192.168.1.0" represents your inside network address based on your firewall's current configuration. If your firewall is configured differently, adjust your settings as needed. Remember to use commands like show ip and show interface to get the necessary information to complete this exercise.)
2. Configure a password for Telnet access:
   `ciscoasa(config)# passwd cisco <enter>`
3. Telnet sessions have a default timeout value of five minutes. Set your appliance timeout value to 10 minutes with this command:

```
ciscoasa(config)# telnet timeout 10 <enter>
```

Test your configuration by attempting to establish a Telnet session from your management workstation using PuTTY:

4. Open PuTTY (if you already have PuTTY open, right-click on the title bar and choose *New Session...*

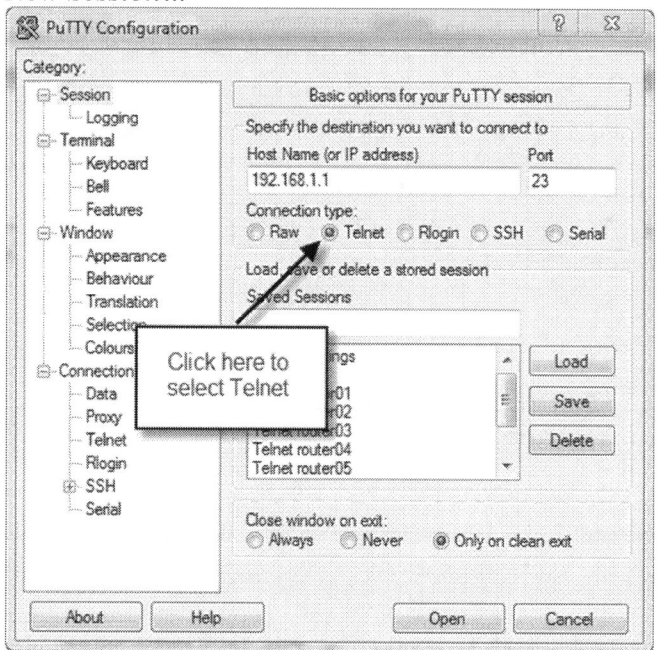

5. In the Host Name (or IP address) field, enter the IP address of your ASA's inside interface (192.168.1.1).
6. Log on with the password *cisco*. If the connection is not successful, review your settings paying particular attention to typographical errors. Make certain that the statement in which you tell the ASA which addresses to accept is correctly configured for your inside network and that you specified the inside interface.

Disconnecting Telnet Sessions

You can disconnect Telnet- sessions with the command `kill [session #]`. Use the command `who` to see active Telnet sessions.

Hands-On Exercise 4.1.2: Configuring and Using SSH (Secure Shell)

In this exercise, you will configure SSH on your appliance. You will then attempt to connect to the appliance using SSH.

1. Generate an RSA keypair with the following command:
   ```
   asa(config)# crypto key generate rsa modulus 1024 <enter>
   ```
   (The modulus represents the key length, in this case 1024 bits.)
2. The firewall will ask if you want to replace the existing RSA keypair. Confirm by entering `yes`.

3. As with Telnet, you must specify the address(es) from which your appliance will accept inbound connections:
   `asa(config)# `**`ssh 192.168.0.0 255.255.0.0 inside`**` <enter>`
   (This statement will allow any host whose IP address begins with 192.168 to connect via SSH to your firewall's inside interface. In a real world setting, a more restrictive configuration would be appropriate.)

4. In the past, PIX firewalls and ASA security appliances used a default username of *pix* if no username was configured. Starting with software version 9.x, a username and password must be explicitly configured with the following command:
   `ciscoasa(config)# `**`username testuser password p@ss1234`**
   `<enter>`

5. Enable AAA authentication for SSH with the following command:
   `asa(config)# `**`aaa authentication ssh console LOCAL`**

6. Set the timeout value to ten minutes for SSH connections:
   `asa(config)# `**`ssh timeout 10`**` <enter>`

7. When you are finished, save the configuration to flash memory:
   `asa(config)# `**`write memory`**` <enter>`

Test the SSH Configuration

Attempt to connect to your appliance by using PuTTY:

1. Ensure that the radio button labeled SSH is selected in the PuTTY window. In the field labeled Host Name (or IP address), enter the inside IP address of your security appliance. Click the button labeled Open.

2. In the Security Warning window that appears, click Yes to accept the key. (On a production system, you should confirm that you are connecting to the system you intended to before accepting the key.)

3. Log on with the username *testuser* and the password *p@ss1234*. If the connection is not successful, confirm that you have correctly entered the username and password. Review your appliances configuration using privileged mode commands such as show run ssh.

4. Now that you have made additional changes to your configuration, save it to flash memory and back it up to your TFTP server using the procedures you learned earlier:
   `asa# `**`wr`**` <enter>`
   `asa# `**`copy run tftp://192.168.1.5/config_ssh.txt`**` <enter>`
   (where 192.168.1.5 is the IP address of your TFTP server)

Disconnecting SSH Sessions

You can disconnect SSH sessions with the command **`ssh disconnect [session #]`**. Use **`show ssh sessions`** to see active SSH sessions.

Hands-On Exercise 5.1: Creating Banners on the Security Appliance

In the following exercise, you will create MOTD, login, and EXEC banners. After configuring the banners, you will test the configuration by logging on in different ways to observe which banners display.

1. In *global configuration mode*, enter the following commands:
   ```
   ciscoasa(config)# banner motd This is the MOTD banner <enter>
   ciscoasa(config)# banner login This is the login banner <enter>
   ciscoasa(config)# banner exec This is the EXEC banner <enter>
   ```

2. Display the banners you just created with the following command:
   ```
   ciscoasa(config)# show run banner <enter>
   ```

3. Type exit repeatedly until you are logged out of your security appliance.

Test the Banner Configuration

1. Notice which banners are displayed with the login prompt.

2. Enter privileged mode and notice which banners are displayed.

3. From your management workstation, start a Telnet session and again observe which banners are displayed. When you are finished, exit the Telnet session.

4. Also from your management workstation, start an SSH session to observe which banners are displayed. If the SSH session fails, review your configuration to see if you can identify the cause of the problem.

5. When you are finished, exit the SSH session.

6. Backup your configuration to your TFTP server using the procedures learned previously.
   ```
   ciscoasa# wr <enter>
   ciscoasa# copy run tftp://192.168.1.5/config_banners.txt <enter>
   ```
   (where 192.168.1.5 is the IP address of your TFTP server)

Hands-On Exercise 5.2: Configuring Usernames and Local Authentication

Configuring usernames is part of implementing AAA (Authentication, Authorization, and Accounting) in that you can specify who can gain access to the security appliance, what they are allowed to do, and later review what they did. In this exercise, you will configure usernames in the local database and specify levels of access.

Building the Configuration in the ASDM

1. On your management workstation, click on Start, then click on Run. In the Run dialog window, enter *https://192.168.1.1* (where 192.168.1.1 is your ASA's inside interface address) and press Enter. (Note the use of "s" in the protocol, identifying the connection as requiring SSL security.)
2. Use a blank username and the password *p@ss5678*. Click through the security warnings to open the ASDM.
3. Ensure that ASDM is configured to allow you to preview commands before sending them to the device by clicking on the *Tools* menu in the menu bar of ASDM. Click on *Preferences* and confirm that the box labeled *Preview commands before sending them to the device* is checked.
4. In the ASDM console menu, click on *Configuration*. On the menu on the left side of the window, click on *Device Management*. Expand *Users/AAA* and click on *User Accounts*.
5. In the *User Accounts* window, click on *Add*.
6. In the *Add User Account* window, change the default username to *user3*. Enter the password *p@ss1234* and confirm it.
7. Under *Access Restriction*, set the privilege level to *3* and click *OK*.
8. Repeat steps 5 and 6, changing the default username to *user5*. Enter the password *p@ss1234* and confirm it.
9. Set the privilege level for user5 to *5*.
10. Repeat steps 5 and 6 again, this time changing the default username to *user15*. Enter the password *p@ss1234* and confirm it.
11. Set the privilege level for user15 to *15*.
12. When you are finished, at the bottom of the *User Accounts* window, click *Apply*. In the *Preview CLI Commands* window, review the changes and click *Send* to send the changes to the appliance.

In order to enforce authentication, you must also make the following changes:

13. Under *Device Management>Users/AAA* (on the left-hand side of your screen), select *AAA Access*.
14. On the *Authentication* tab, check the box labeled *Enable* to require authentication for administrator access to the appliance. Accept the default *Server Group Local*.
15. In the *Require authentication for the following types of connections* section, check the boxes labeled *SSH* and *Telnet* and accept the default *Server Group Local*. (In a real-world setting, you would probably want to enforce authentication for ASDM as well.)
16. At the bottom of the window, click on *Apply*. In the *Preview CLI Commands* window, review the changes and click *Send* to send the changes to the appliance.
17. Under the *Authorization* tab, check the box labeled *Enable* and click on the button labeled *Set ASDM Defined User Roles*.

18. The *ASDM Defined User Roles* window will appear. Notice that it associates various commands in the three left-hand columns with privilege levels displayed in the far right-hand column. The privilege levels represent *Monitor (level 3)*, *Read Only (level 5)*, and *Admin (level 15)*. Level 15 commands are not displayed because Admin already has full access. When you have finished reviewing the settings, click *Yes* to allow ASDM to configure commands with the indicated privilege levels. Be sure to click *Apply* and *Send* to send the commands to the security appliance.
(Note: In a real world setting, you could use this tool to set very specific access-levels for users at any command level.)

Testing the Configuration

19. Use PuTTY to open an SSH session to the ASA. (Use PuTTY to connect to 192.168.1.1.)

20. Notice that it now prompts you for a username. Enter *user3* with the password *p@ss1234*.

21. You are logged in to the device in User Mode. Enter *enable* and the password *p@ss1234* to change to Privileged Mode.

22. Enter the command *show running-config*. What happens?

23. The command should fail with an invalid input error because user3 is associated with command level three and command level three does not include authorization to run the *show running-config* command.

24. Type *exit* to close PuTTY. Re-open the SSH session to 192.168.1.1, but this time, enter the username *user5* with the password *p@ss1234*.

25. Enter *enable* and the password *p@ss1234* to change to Privileged Mode.

26. Enter the command *show running-config*. What happens now?

27. The command should be successful, because user5 is associated with command level five and command level five includes authorization to run the *show running-config* command.

28. Enter the command *config t*. What happens?

29. The command should fail with an invalid input error because user5 is associated with command level five and command level five does not include authorization to run the *configure terminal* command.

30. Type *exit* to close the PuTTY SSH session. Re-open it as before, but this time, enter the username *user15* with the password *p@ss1234*.

31. Enter *enable* and the password *p@ss1234* to change to Privileged Mode.

32. Enter the command *show running-config*. What happens now?

33. The command should be successful, because user15 is associated with command level fifteen and command level fifteen includes authorization to run the *show running-config* command.

34. Enter the command *config t*. What happens now?

35. The command should be successful, because user15 is associated with command level fifteen and command level fifteen includes authorization to run the *configure terminal* command.
36. Now that you have made additional changes to your configuration, save it to flash memory and back it up to your TFTP server using the procedures you learned earlier.
    ```
    ciscoasa# wr <enter>
    ciscoasa# copy run tftp://192.168.1.5/config_aaa_priv.txt
    <enter>
    ```
    (where 192.168.1.5 is the IP address of your TFTP server)

Hands-On Exercise 5.3: Configuring ASA Authentication through Active Directory

In this exercise, you will configure your ASA security appliance to authenticate SSH users against a Microsoft Active Directory domain controller.

Prerequisites

- A Windows domain controller configured with Network Policy and Access Server role and the Network Policy Server (for more information, including a step-by-step guide, see the tutorial at http://www.soundtraining.net/i-t-tutorials/cisco-tutorials).
- An Active Directory user account on the Windows domain controller for user01 with a password of p@ss1234
- User user01's Dial-In Remote Access permission on the Windows domain controller must be set to Allow Access.

Configuration Steps

1. In a terminal window, enter *global configuration mode*:

    ```
    ciscoasa>en
    Password: p@ss5678
    ciscoasa# conf t
    ciscoasa(config)#
    ```

2. In global configuration mode, specify the authentication protocol, create the authentication group (RADIUSSERVERS), identify the interface to which the authentication server is connected (outside), specify the server's IP address, and the key shared between the security appliance and the authentication server (p@ss5678). (Note, each of the following commands should be entered on a single line.):

    ```
    ciscoasa(config)# aaa-server RADIUSSERVERS protocol radius
    ciscoasa(config-aaa-server-group)# aaa-server RADIUSSERVERS
    (outside) host 192.168.0.1
    ```

    (where 192.168.0.1 is the IP address of the RADIUS server)

```
ciscoasa(config-aaa-server-host)# key p@ss5678
ciscoasa(config-aaa-server-host)# exit
```

3. While still in global configuration mode, specify the services you wish to have authenticated through radius, making sure to include local authentication as a backup in case the authentication server is not available:

   ```
   ciscoasa(config)# aaa authentication ssh console RADIUSSERVERS LOCAL
   ```

4. If you receive an error in entering the above commands, check to be sure that aaa authentication is not already configured with the following command:

   ```
   ciscoasa# show run aaa
   ```

5. You should see output similar to this:

   ```
   aaa authentication enable console LOCAL
   aaa authentication serial console LOCAL
   aaa authentication ssh console LOCAL
   aaa authentication telnet console LOCAL
   aaa authorization command LOCAL
   ```

6. If aaa authentication is already configured (perhaps from a previous exercise), you must first remove it before configuring aaa authentication through RADIUS. In the Cisco command-line, you can remove configuration statements by preceding the same statement used to enable a configuration with the modifier "no". For example, you can remove the previous aaa ssh configuration with this command:

   ```
   ciscoasa(config)# no aaa authentication ssh console LOCAL
   ```

7. When you have completed the configuration, log off the firewall and, using SSH, attempt to re-login as *user01* with a password of *p@ss1234*. Your login should be successful.

Hands-On Exercise 6.1: Reconfiguring Your DHCP Server

In this exercise, you will use the CLI to reconfigure your firewall's internal IP address and its DHCP address pool.

Assign a Different IP Address to Your Inside Interface

Use the following table to determine the particular addresses to use in this exercise, based on the name of your ASA (from the label on the top):

ASA	Inside Interface Address	dhcpd Address Range
asa01	192.168.101.1	192.168.101.6-192.168.101.37
asa02	192.168.102.1	192.168.102.6-192.168.102.37
asa03	192.168.103.1	192.168.103.6-192.168.103.37
asa04	192.168.104.1	192.168.104.6-192.168.104.37

| asa05 | 192.168.105.1 | 192.168.105.6-192.168.105.37 |
| asa06 | 192.168.106.1 | 192.168.106.6-192.168.106.37 |

1. Log in as user15 with the password p@ss1234.

2. Assign a new IP address for your firewall's inside interface using the following commands:

   ```
   ciscoasa# conf t
   ciscoasa(config)# interface vlan1
   ciscoasa(config-if)# ip address 192.168.101.1
   ```

3. Notice that the change fails due to a conflict with your DHCP address pool. In order to make these changes, you must first remove the existing DHCP scope. The easiest way to do so is by showing the current scope with the following command:

   ```
   ciscoasa(config)# show run dhcpd
   ```

4. You'll see a line similar to this:

   ```
   dhcpd address 192.168.1.6-192.168.1.30 inside
   ```

5. Use your mouse to capture (copy) the line. In your firewall's command-line interface, enter the word "no", followed by a space, then paste the above line into the CLI so that it looks similar to this:

   ```
   ciscoasa(config)# no dhcpd address 192.168.1.6-192.168.1.37 inside
   ```

   (Note: If the above command fails, check the actual dhcp configuration on your firewall with the show run dhcpd command. You may need to adjust the starting and ending addresses in the pool to match your firewall's actual configuration.)

6. You should now be able to change your firewall's internal IP address with the following commands. Notice that the firewall does not require you to enter a subnet mask. It automatically appends the default mask based on the class of address.

   ```
   ciscoasa(config)# interface vlan1
   ciscoasa(config-if)# ip address [USE INSIDE INTERFACE ADDRESS FROM ABOVE TABLE]
   ```

7. Save your configuration to flash memory:

   ```
   ciscoasa(config-if)# wr
   ```

Configure a New DHCP Pool

1. Configure a new DHCP pool for clients on your inside interface with the following command:

   ```
   ciscoasa(config)# dhcpd address [USE DHCPD ADDRESS RANGE FOR YOUR ASA FROM THE ABOVE TABLE] inside
   ```

2. Add a default route (also known as a "default gateway" or a "gateway of last resort" using DHCP option 3 (the standard DHCP option number for the default router)

   ciscoasa(config)# **dhcpd option 3 ip [USE THE INSIDE INTERFACE ADDRESS FOR YOUR ASA FROM THE ABOVE TABLE]**

3. Enable the new pool with the following command:

   ciscoasa(config)# **dhcpd enable inside**

4. In the command-line interface of your management workstation, release and renew your computer's IP address.

   ipconfig /release
   ipconfig /renew

   You should immediately see a new IP address from the newly configured pool.

   Now that you have made additional changes to your configuration, save it to flash memory and back it up to your TFTP server using the procedures you learned earlier
   ciscoasa(config)# **wr**

   ciscoasa(config)# **copy run tftp://[YOUR COMPUTER'S ADDRESS]/config_dhcpd.txt**
   (Note: You may need to restart your TFTP server before this command will work.)

Hands-On Exercise 8.1: Site-to-Site VPNs

In this exercise, you will simulate a VPN connecting two geographically separate offices across the public Internet. Each security appliance can function as both initiator and/or responder. This exercise will be completed using the Command Line Interface (CLI).

You will peer with a partner ASA appliance to complete this exercise.

Hands-On Exercise 8.1.1: Save the Appliance's Current Running Configuration to Flash Memory

Enter the following command to save your current configuration to flash memory:

asa#write mem

IMPORTANT: Do not save your configuration to flash memory again during the VPN exercises. After the VPN exercises, you will reload your ASA to return to a pristine configuration.

Hands-On Exercise 8.1.2: Attempt the Remote Connection

Note: In order for this exercise to work, you must either allow ICMP through the Windows firewall or disable the firewall. In a real world setting, you should not normally disable host-based firewalls. The procedure to manage the Windows firewall varies based on your operating system. In Windows 7, go to your Control Panel, then System and Security, then Windows Firewall.

1. On your management workstation, start a continuous ping to the remote host (your partner's management workstation):
   a. Click on Start, then click on Run (or use the key combination of Win+R).
   b. In the Run dialog window, enter "cmd" to open a command window.
2. Ask your partner for the IP address of his/her management workstation. Then, type the following command:

   `ping w.x.y.z -t`
   (where "w.x.y.z" represents the IP address of your partner's management workstation and the –t option makes it a continuous ping until you stop it with the key combination of CTRL+C.)
3. Notice that the ping is not successful.
4. Move the command window to the edge of your screen where it will be visible while you configure your appliance and leave the ping running.

Building the Tunnel

5. Enter *global configuration mode*

   `ciscoasa# config t`
6. Enable ISAKMP on the outside interface

   `ciscoasa(config)# crypto isakmp enable outside`

Create the Network Objects

Network objects are simply a way of identifying individual hosts or groups of hosts on a network. They can be reused in various configurations.

ASA	Inside Subnet and Mask	Outside Interface Address
asa01	192.168.101.0 255.255.255.0	192.168.0.101
asa02	192.168.102.0 255.255.255.0	192.168.0.102
asa03	192.168.103.0 255.255.255.0	192.168.0.103
asa04	192.168.104.0 255.255.255.0	192.168.0.104
asa05	192.168.105.0 255.255.255.0	192.168.0.105
asa06	192.168.106.0 255.255.255.0	192.168.0.106

7. Create a network object for your inside subnet. Refer to the above table for your inside subnet address and mask.

   `ciscoasa(config)# object network net-local`

```
ciscoasa(config-network-object)# subnet [YOUR INSIDE SUBNET
AND MASK]
```

8. Create a network object for the remote subnet. Refer to the above table for your partner's inside subnet address and mask.

```
ciscoasa(config-network-object)# object network net-remote
ciscoasa(config-network-object)# subnet [YOUR PARTNER'S
INSIDE SUBNET AND MASK]
ciscoasa(config-network-object)# exit
```

Create an Access-Control List

9. Create an access-control list to identify the traffic flow from your inside subnet to the remote inside subnet:

```
ciscoasa(config)# access-list outside_1_cryptomap permit ip
object net-local object net-remote
```

Create and Configure the Tunnel Group

10. Create a tunnel-group to identify the remote firewall's outside interface and the type of VPN (ipsec, lan-to-lan):

```
ciscoasa(config)# tunnel-group [PARTNER'S OUTSIDE IP
ADDRESS] type ipsec-l2l
```
(Note: l2l is the letter "l" as in lan-2-lan, not the number "one".)

11. Create a tunnel-group to set tunnel attributes including the shared key and keepalives:

```
ciscoasa(config)# tunnel-group [PARTNER'S OUTSIDE IP
ADDRESS] ipsec-attributes
ciscoasa(config-tunnel-ipsec)# pre-shared-key p@ss5678
ciscoasa(config-tunnel-ipsec)# isakmp keepalive threshold
10 retry 2
ciscoasa(config-tunnel-ipsec)# exit
```

Configure Phase 1

Phase one is where the two firewalls handshake to manage the key exchange. This portion of the configuration uses asynchronous key cryptography.

12. Create an isakmp policy to specify the authentication method

```
ciscoasa(config)# crypto isakmp policy 10 authentication
pre-share
```

13. Create an isakmp policy to specify the encryption algorithm

```
ciscoasa(config)# crypto isakmp policy 10 encrypt 3des
```

14. Create an isakmp policy to specify the hashing algorithm

```
ciscoasa(config)# crypto isakmp policy 10 hash sha
```

15. Create an isakmp policy to specify the Diffie-Hellman group

```
ciscoasa(config)# crypto isakmp policy 10 group 2
```

16. Create an isakmp policy to specify the key lifetime

```
ciscoasa(config)# crypto isakmp policy 10 lifetime 86400
```

Configure Phase 2

Phase two is the configuration used for the actual tunnel. It is based on synchronous key cryptography.

17. Create an ipsec policy to specify the encryption and hashing algorithms to be used on the tunnel:

    ```
    ciscoasa(config)# crypto ipsec transform-set ESP-3DES-SHA esp-3des esp-sha-hmac
    ```

18. Create a crypto map entry to identify an already configured access-control list that identifies the traffic flow(s) to be protected

    ```
    ciscoasa(config)# crypto map outside_map 1 match address outside_1_cryptomap
    ```

19. Create a crypto map entry to enable perfect forward secrecy using Diffie-Hellman group One. (PFS periodically generates new session keys for encrypted messages, thus making it more difficult for an attacker to use captured keys to decrypt a message.)

    ```
    ciscoasa(config)# crypto map outside_map 1 set pfs group1
    ```

20. Create a crypto map entry to identify the remote firewall's outside interface IP address:

    ```
    ciscoasa(config)# crypto map outside_map 1 set  peer [PARTNER'S OUTSIDE IP ADDRESS]
    ```

21. Create a crypto map entry to identify the transform-set which will be applied to the tunnel

    ```
    ciscoasa(config)# crypto map outside_map 1 set  transform-set  ESP-3DES-SHA
    ```

22. Apply the crypto map to the outside interface

    ```
    ciscoasa(config)# crypto map outside_map interface outside
    ```

Configure NAT

23. Create a NAT statement to prevent tunnel traffic from being NAT'ed (that's the number 1, not the letter "l").

    ```
    ciscoasa(config)# nat (inside,outside) 1 source static net-local net-local destination static net-remote net-remote
    ```

Configure a Default Route

24. Create a default route:

```
ciscoasa(config)# route outside 0 0 192.168.0.1
```

(Note: As elsewhere in this workshop, 192.168.0.1 is the default gateway for the lab. In the real world, use the gateway address for your network. If you are working independently, the default route is probably provided by your ISP.)

Hands-On Exercise 8.1.3: Wrapping up the Site-to-Site VPN Exercise

Now that you have made additional changes to your configuration, back it up using the procedures learned earlier:

```
asa# copy run tftp://[YOUR COMPUTER'S IP ADDRESS]/config_vpn_l21.txt
```

When you and your partner are both finished, reload your appliances.

Hands-On Exercise 8.2: Configuring a Cisco AnyConnect Remote Access VPN

This is a basic VPN configuration for remote workers. In this exercise, you will configure your security appliance to accept inbound remote access connections from clients running the Cisco AnyConnect VPN client software. This exercise will use the ASDM for configuration. When configured to accept inbound remote access connections, the security appliance functions only as a responder.

Hands-On Exercise 8.2.1: Building the Basic AnyConnect Configuration

Building this configuration requires the following steps:
- Create a connection profile
- Choose VPN protocols and certificate
- Add a VPN client image
- Configure authentication
- Configure a DHCP pool for remote clients
- Configure name resolution servers
- Enable NAT exemption
- Configure AnyConnect client deployment

Prerequisite

Download the AnyConnect client from the classroom FTP server. Your instructor will tell you which image to download, but in general, you should use the most recent image available.

Copy the AnyConnect image into your device's flash memory using TFTP.

Configuration Steps

1. Connect to the ASDM (Adaptive Security Device Manager) by entering https://[YOUR DEVICE'S INSIDE ADDRESS] in a browser. Authenticate as needed.
2. Click on *Wizards*, then *VPN Wizards*, and then *AnyConnect VPN Wizard*.
3. The AnyConnect VPN Wizard opens. Click *Next*.
4. Enter *RemoteUsers* for the Connection Profile Name, accept the default VPN Access Interface of *outside* and click *Next*.
5. In the VPN Protocols page, accept the default protocols (SSL and IPSec). A certificate is required, so click the button labeled *Manage*.
    a. Under *Manage Identity Certificates*, click *Add*.
    b. Under *Add Identity Certificate*, choose *Add a new identity certificate* and check the box labeled *Generate self-signed certificate*.
    c. Click the button labeled *Advanced*.
    d. Under *Advanced Options*, confirm or enter your device's fully qualified domain name:
    `[YOUR DEVICE'S NAME].soundtraining.local`
    (For example, if your ASA's name is asa06, the fully qualified domain name will be *asa06.soundtraining.local*.)
    e. Click *OK*
    f. Back in the *Add Identity Certificate* window, change the CN to match the fully qualified domain name you just configured.
    g. Click *Add Certificate*.
    h. Click *Send*.
    i. Click *OK* when you see the message *Enrollment succeeded*.
    j. Click *OK* in the *Manage Identity Certificates* window.
    k. Notice that the certificate you just created and installed is visible in the Wizard window. Click *Next*.
6. In the *Client Images* window, add the AnyConnect client image by clicking the button labeled *Add*.
    a. Click the button labeled *Browse flash* and select the most recent AnyConnect client image. Click *OK*.
    b. Click *OK*.
    c. The image you just added should be visible in the *Client Images* window.
    d. Click *Next*.
7. In the *Authentication Methods* window, add the user **vpnuser** and the password **p@ss1234**. Confirm the password, click *Add* and click *Next*.

8. In the *Client Address Assignment* window, under the *IPv4 Address Pool* tab, click *New*.

9. In the *Add IPv4 Pool* window, enter the following parameters:
   a. Name: `net-10`
   b. Starting IP address: `10.0.0.1`
   c. Ending IP address: `10.0.0.10`
   d. Subnet Mask: `255.255.255.0`

10. Click *OK,* then click *Next*.

11. In the *Network Name Resolutions Servers* window, enter the following parameters:
    a. DNS Servers: `192.168.0.1`
    b. WINS Servers: Leave blank
    c. Domain Name: `soundtraining.local`

12. Click *Next*.

13. In the *NAT Exempt* window, check the box to *Exempt VPN traffic from Network Address Translation*. Click *Next*.

14. Under *AnyConnect Client Deployment*, accept the defaults and click *Next*.

15. On the *Summary* page, click *Finish*.

16. On the *Preview* page, click *Send*.

17. When you're finished, ask your instructor to test your configuration by connecting to your VPN.

Hands-On Exercise 8.2.2: Configuring ASA VPN Authentication through Active Directory Using RADIUS

In this exercise, you will configure your ASA security appliance to authenticate SSH users against a Microsoft Active Directory domain controller running Windows Server 2012. You can use either the ASDM (Adaptive Security Device Manager) of the command-line to perform this configuration. I find it's easier to do these steps in the command-line, so that's what I'll show you. There is a wizard in the ASDM to help you configure a remote-access VPN, if that's your preference.

Prerequisites

- Administrator-level access to an ASA security appliance with an AnyConnect Remote-Access VPN configured. In this tutorial, you will learn how to add RADIUS authentication to an existing VPN configuration.
- An Active Directory user account (in the example, the user account is user01).
- A Windows Server computer configured to support RADIUS. (See our online tutorial at www.soundtraining.net for the steps to build such a configuration.)

Configuration Steps

1. In *global configuration mode*, create an AAA (authentication, authorization, and accounting) server group, specifying RADIUS as the protocol:
   `asa01(config)#` **`aaa-server RADIUSSERVERS protocol radius`**

2. Identify the location of the RADIUS server:
   `asa01(config-aaa-server-group)#` **`aaa-server RADIUSSERVERS (outside) host 192.168.0.1`**

3. Create the key that will be shared with the RADIUS server. (On the Windows Server 2012 RADIUS server, this is known as the *pre-shared key*.)
   `asa01(config-aaa-server-host)#` **`key p@ss5678`**

4. Edit the tunnel-group associated with the ASA's VPN users. (In the example, the tunnel-group name is *RemoteUsers*. If you don't know the tunnel-group's name, you can use the command show run tunnel to display it.)
   `asa01(config-aaa-server-host)#` **`tunnel-group RemoteUsers general-attributes`**

5. Add the authentication-server-group you created in the previous step. (In this example, it's RADIUSSERVERS.)
   `asa01(config-tunnel-general)#` **`authentication-server-group RADIUSSERVERS LOCAL`**
   (Note: Be sure to include the LOCAL statement at the end of the line as a fallback in case the RADIUS server is not reachable. Otherwise, no one will be able to log in.)

6. You can test the configuration from the command-line:
   `asa01#` **`test aaa-server authentication RADIUSSERVERS host 192.168.0.1 username user01 password p@ss1234`**
   (In this example, user01 is an existing Active Directory user account.)

Sample Configuration

```
asa01# conf t
asa01(config)# aaa-server RADIUSSERVERS protocol radius
asa01(config-aaa-server-group)# aaa-server RADIUSSERVERS (inside) host 192.168.101.15
asa01(config-aaa-server-host)# key p@ss5678
asa01(config-aaa-server-host)# show run tunnel
tunnel-group "Account Reps NA" type remote-access
tunnel-group "Account Reps NA" general-attributes
 address-pool net-10
 default-group-policy "GroupPolicy_Account Reps NA"
tunnel-group "Account Reps NA" webvpn-attributes
 group-alias "Account Reps NA" enable
asa01(config-aaa-server-host)# tunnel-group "Account Reps NA" general-attributes
asa01(config-tunnel-general)# authentication-server-group RADIUSSERVERS LOCAL
asa01(config-tunnel-general)#
asa01# test aaa-server authentication RADIUSSERVERS host 192.168.101.15 username user01 password p@ss1234
INFO: Attempting Authentication test to IP address <192.168.101.15> (timeout: 12 seconds)
INFO: Authentication Successful
asa01#
```

Hands-On Exercise 8.2.3: Configuring Kerberos Authentication

1. In global configuration mode, issue the following commands to connect to the AD server:
   ```
   aaa-server ADSERVERS protocol Kerberos
   aaa-server ADSERVERS (outside) host 192.168.0.1
   kerberos-realm SOUNDTRAINING.LOCAL
   ```
2. Issue the following commands to enable authentication for VPN users:
   ```
   tunnel-group RemoteUsers general-attributes
   authentication-server-group ADSERVERS LOCAL
   ```
3. Test the configuration with the following command:
   ```
   test aaa-server authentication ADSERVERS host 192.168.0.1
   username user01 password p@ss1234
   ```

Hands-On Exercise 8.2.4: Configuring LDAP Authentication

1. In global configuration mode, issue the following commands to connect to the LDAP server:
   ```
   aaa-server LDAPSERVERS (outside) host 192.168.0.1
    ldap-base-dn dc=soundtraining,dc=local
    ldap-scope subtree
    ldap-naming-attribute sAMAccountName
    ldap-login-password p@ss5678
    ldap-login-dn
   cn=administrator,cn=Users,dc=soundtraining,dc=local
    server-type auto-detect
   ```
2. Issue the following commands to enable authentication for VPN users:
   tunnel-group "RemoteUsers" general-attributes
   ```
   tunnel-group RemoteUsers general-attributes
   authentication-server-group LDAPSERVERS LOCAL
   ```
3. Test the configuration with the following command:
   ```
   test aaa-server authentication LDAPSERVERS host 192.168.0.1
   username user01 password p@ss1234
   ```

Hands-On Exercise 9.1: Configuring a DMZ

In this exercise, you will configure a DMZ VLAN in which the hosts, including shared printers, on the DMZ VLAN are accessible to hosts on the business VLAN, but not the other way around.

1. Reload your ASA with the privileged mode command "`reload`" to return it to a pristine configuration. (Remember what we did right before all of the VPN exercises?) Do NOT save the existing configuration.

2. On your management workstation, click on Start, then click Run. Enter `https://[YOUR ASA'S INSIDE INTERFACE ADDRESS]` in the Run dialog window to connect to your ASA. Follow the prompts, using the password *p@ss5678* when required to connect to the ASDM console.

3. Click through the security warnings in order to establish a connection with the ASDM (Adaptive Security Device Manager).

4. Navigate to Configuration>Interfaces. Notice in the Interfaces window that there are two interfaces already configured: An inside interface and an outside interface. If your device has more than two interfaces configured, delete any interface NOT named "inside" or "outside".

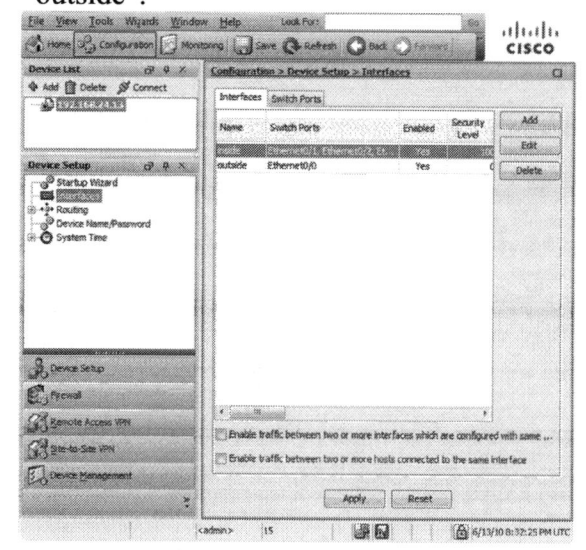

5. You will now build a DMZ from scratch. On the right-hand side of the console, click on the button labeled Add.

6. The Add Interface window appears. In the Switch Ports section, under Available Switch Ports, select Ethernet0/3 and click the button labeled Add to add Switch Port Ethernet 0/3 to the Selected Switch Ports list on the right. Click OK if you receive a Change Switch Port warning.

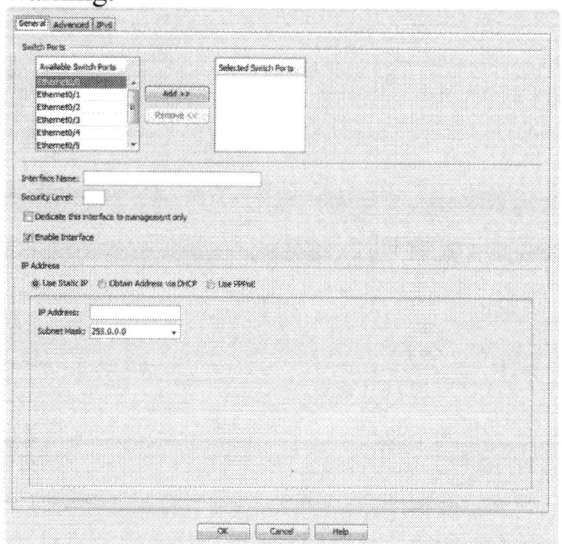

7. Repeat step five for Switch Port Ethernet 0/4.

8. Ensure that the check box labeled Enable Interface is checked.

9. If your ASA 5505 is licensed with the Base License, it supports only two fully functional interfaces. By configuring a third interface (the DMZ VLAN), you will exceed the licensed number of interfaces unless you limit access from one of the three interfaces to one of the

other interfaces. In this exercise, you will prevent hosts on the DMZ VLAN from accessing resources on the Inside VLAN.

10. At the top of the Add Interface window, click on the Advanced tab.

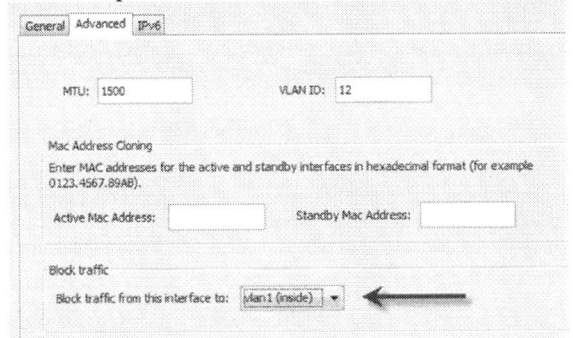

11. In the middle of the window, in the Block Traffic section, use the pull-down menu to block traffic from this interface to vlan1 (inside).

12. Return to the General page by clicking the tab at the top of the page.

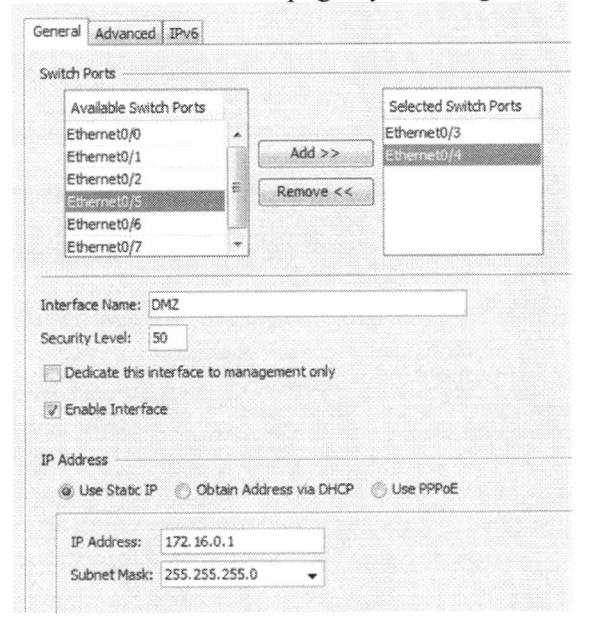

13. Enter DMZ for the Interface Name.

14. Enter 50 for the Security Level.

15. In the IP Address section, ensure that the radio button labeled Use Static IP is selected.

16. Enter 172.16.0.1 for the IP address and select 255.255.255.0 for the subnet mask.

17. At the bottom of the window, click the button labeled OK

18. At the bottom of the window, click the button labeled Apply. Review the commands in the Preview CLI Commands window, then click Send.

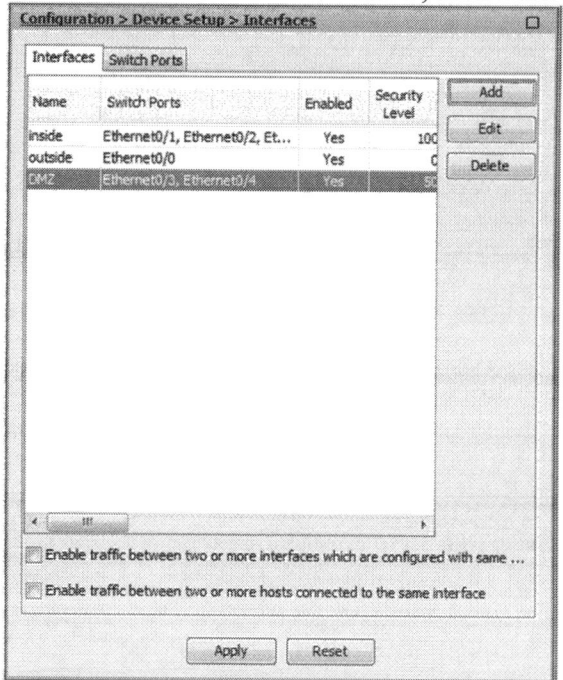

19. Exit from the ASDM.

20. Test your DMZ VLAN by connecting your management workstation's Ethernet cable to SwitchPort 0/3 on your ASA.

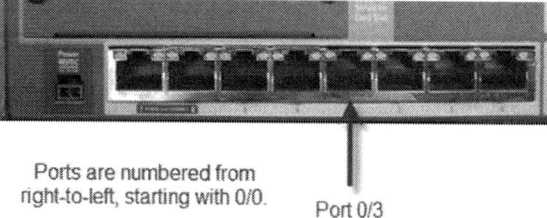

Ports are numbered from right-to-left, starting with 0/0. Port 0/3

21. On your PC, click on Start>Run and enter `http://www.soundtraining.local` in the Run dialog window to attempt an HTTP connection with a Web server. What happens?

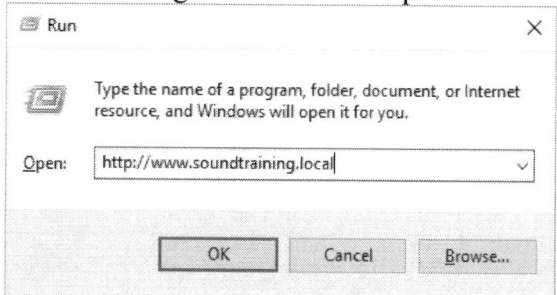

22. In the command window, type `ipconfig` to display your computer's TCP/IP settings. Recall that the DMZ VLAN's IP address is 172.16.0.1. Notice that your computer is on a different subnet.

23. In order for your computer to use the DMZ VLAN interface, it must be configured with an IP address on the 172.16.0 subnet. You could configure it statically, but static IP address configuration is not a scalable solution and DHCP is a preferred solution. In the next few steps, you will configure a DHCP scope on your ASA for the 172.16.0 subnet.

24. Switch your computer's Ethernet cable back to port Ethernet 0/1 on your security appliance.

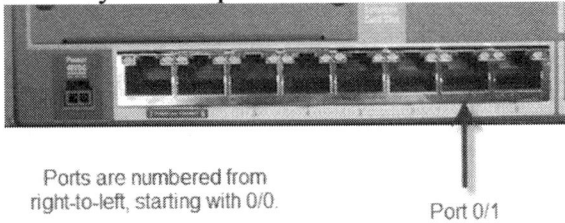

    Ports are numbered from right-to-left, starting with 0/0.

    Port 0/1

25. In the ASDM console, in the menu bar at the top of the console, click on Configuration, then in the lower left-hand corner of the console window click on Device Management. In the properties list, expand DHCP and select DHCP Server.

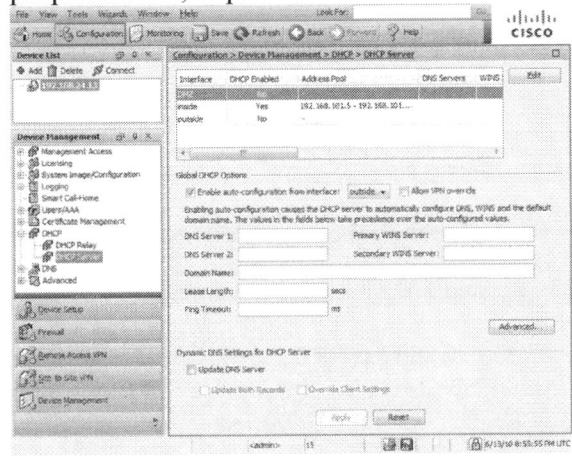

26. Notice in the DHCP Server window, in the DHCP Server section, the three interfaces are listed, but only one has an address pool configured.

27. Select the DMZ interface and click the Edit button immediately to the right of the DHCP Server section. The Edit DHCP Server window will appear.

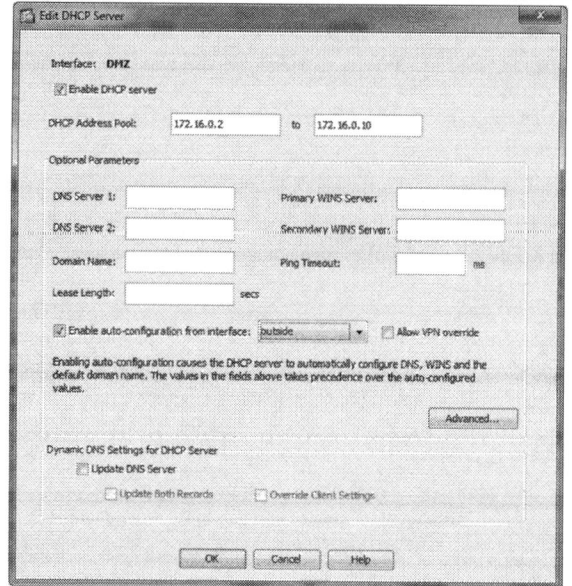

28. Check the box labeled Enable DHCP Server.

29. For the DHCP Address Pool settings, enter 172.16.0.2 to 172.16.0.10.

30. Toward the bottom of the Optional Parameters section, check the box labeled Enable auto-configuration on interface: and select Outside from the pull-down menu.

31. Click the button labeled Advanced…

32. On the Advanced DHCP Options page, select Option Code 3(Router).

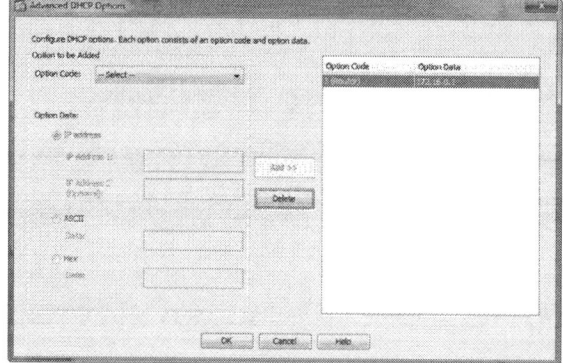

33. In the Option Data section, in the field labeled Router 1, enter 172.16.0.1. Leave the field labeled Router2 blank.

34. Click Add, then click OK.

35. Click OK at the bottom of the Edit DHCP Server window.

36. Click Apply at the bottom of the Configuration Properties window and click Send to send the changes to the security appliance.

37. Test your DHCP Server configuration. Reconnect your management workstation to SwitchPort 0/3 on your security appliance, click Start, then click Run. In the Run dialog window, type `cmd` to open a command window.

38. In the command window, type ipconfig to display your current IP address.

39. Now, type `ipconfig /renew` to request a new IP address. After a few seconds, you should see an IP address of 172.16.0.2 and a default gateway of 172.16.0.1.

40. Attempt to connect to a website. On your PC, click on Start>Run and enter http://www.soundtraining.local in the Run dialog window. The connection is still unsuccessful, because Port Address Translation has not been configured for the DMZ yet.

41. Configure PAT for the DMZ. (In this configuration, "subnet 0 0 represents any IP address and mask. You might want to make a more restrictive statement by explicitly specifying the DMZ subnet.)
```
ciscoasa(config)# object network DMZ_outside
ciscoasa(config-network-object)# subnet 0 0
ciscoasa(config-network-object)# nat (DMZ,outside) dynamic interface
```

In a real-world setting, a DMZ could contain resources such as a printer or a Web server that hosts on the Inside VLAN would need to access. In this section of the exercise, you will configure a computer connected to the DMZ VLAN as a Web server. You will then configure the firewall to allow access to the DMZ VLAN from both the Inside VLAN and the outside VLAN. Hosts on the Inside VLAN will be protected from hosts on the DMZ VLAN because traffic will not be permitted to flow from the DMZ VLAN to the Inside VLAN.

Installing the Abyss Web Server Software

You will now install a Web server application on your management workstation using the following commands. (The Abyss Web server was chosen for this exercise because it is small and quick to install. We have not tested it in a production environment and do not recommend it without testing and evaluation.)

42. On your management workstation, click on Start, then click on Run.

43. In the Run dialog box, enter http://www.aprelium.com/abyssws/download.php

44. On the download page, find and download the correct software for your platform (This exercise does not specifically require the Abyss web server; you can use any web server software you prefer.)

45. Install and configure, using defaults, the Abyss web server software.

46. Following installation, ensure that the web server software is running on your computer.

47. Some PCs may be configured with the Windows firewall (or another firewall such as Zone Alarm). If so, a Windows Security Alert may appear. Click Unblock.

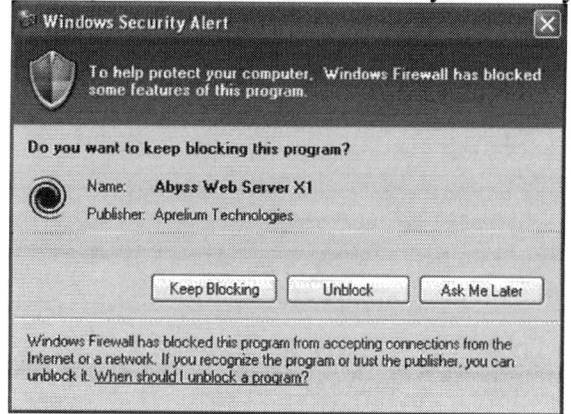

48. Confirm that your webserver is working by clicking Start, then Run. In the Run dialog window, enter http://localhost. You should see the Abyss default page.

Allowing Inside Hosts and Internet Hosts Access to the DMZ Web Server

49. Create the network object web-server-fromOutside for the Web server at 172.16.0.2 and create a static NAT statement to forward www traffic on the outside interface to the host in the DMZ

    ```
    ciscoasa(config)# object network web-server-fromOutside
    ciscoasa(config-network-object)# host 172.16.0.2
    ciscoasa(config-network-object)# nat (DMZ,outside) static interface service tcp www www
    ```

50. Create the network object web-server-fromInside for the Web server at 172.16.0.2 and create a static NAT statement to forward www traffic on the inside interface to the host in the DMZ

    ```
    ciscoasa(config)# object network web-server-fromInside
    ciscoasa(config-network-object)# host 172.16.0.2
    ciscoasa(config-network-object)# nat (DMZ,inside) static interface service tcp www www
    ciscoasa(config)#
    ```

51. Create the ACL OutsidetoDMZ to allow www traffic to flow against the security level from any source to the host at 172.16.0.2 and apply it to inbound traffic on the outside interface.

    ```
    ciscoasa(config)# access-list OutsidetoDMZ extended permit tcp any host 172.16.0.2 eq www
    ciscoasa(config)# access-group OutsidetoDMZ in interface outside
    ```

52. Test the configuration by attempting to connect to the Web server from both the outside network using your ASA's outside address and from the inside network using your ASA's inside address.
53. Now that you have made additional changes to your configuration, save it to flash memory and back it up using the procedures learned earlier:

    ```
    ciscoasa# wr
    ```

    ```
    ciscoasa# copy run tftp://[YOUR PC's IP ADDRESS]/config_dmz.txt
    ```

Hands-On Exercise 9.2: Analyzing Potential Vulnerabilities with Port Scanning

In this exercise, you will use the port scanner nmap (Network Mapper) to identify ports on a host that are open and waiting for connections. You will actually be using Zenmap, the graphical version of nmap.

Warning: Do not attempt port scanning on a production network without written permission from your supervisor. Port scanning can be seen as a reconnaissance attack.

1. In order to run nmap, you must install it along with WinPCap (Windows Packet Capture). Download nmap from http://www.soundtraining.local and install it on your management workstation.
2. Click through the various prompts, accepting the defaults, to complete the installation. (The installation will actually install both WinPCap and nmap.)
3. Start nmap by clicking on Start, mouse over All Programs, then mouse over Nmap, then click on Nmap –Zenmap GUI.
4. Zenmap is the GUI version of Nmap. In the Zenmap window, enter the IP address of your ASA's inside interface. Accept the default profile of "Intense scan", and click the button labeled "Scan". After a few moments, the resulting of the scan will be displayed

in the Nmap output window.

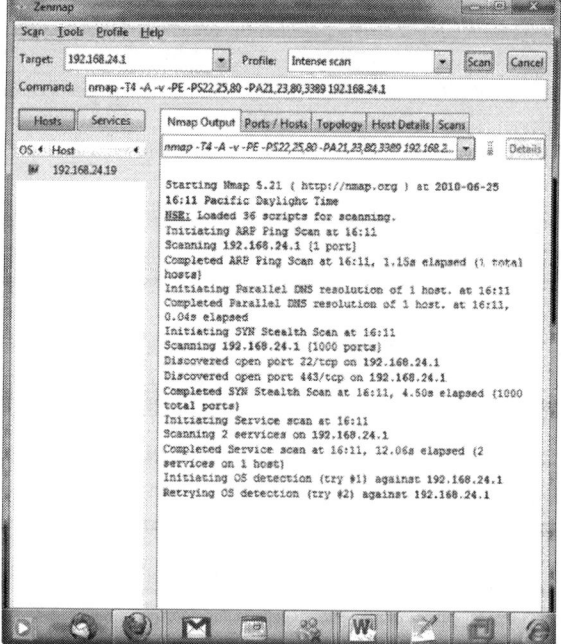

[Screenshot of Zenmap Nmap output window showing scan of 192.168.24.1 with intense scan profile, displaying scan progress including ARP Ping Scan, SYN Stealth Scan discovering open ports 22/tcp and 443/tcp, Service scan, and OS detection attempts.]

5. Wait a few more minutes and Nmap will display information about any services it finds on the targeted host. Most likely, you will only see ports 22 (ssh) and 443 (https) open.
6. If you are working with a partner, connect to the same VLAN as his/her management workstation and perform the same scan against that computer. Have your partner try disabling the Windows firewall on his/her computer and try the scan again. Compare the results. You should see many different services open after disabling the firewall.

Hands-On Exercise 10.1: Filtering Dynamic Content

In this exercise, you will connect to a website constructed with Java applets. You will then implement Java filtering on your security appliance to prevent such applets from running.

Note: Starting with Chrome version 42, release in April 2015, Java applets are no longer supported in the Chrome browser. In order to complete this exercise, Oracle recommends that you use the Internet Explorer or Safari browsers.

1. Connect to the classroom website by pointing your browser to
   http://www.soundtraining.local/applets

2. There are several applets available for you to run, including the applet of the month on the left-hand side of the page. Choose an applet and run it for long enough to see it work.

3. Filter all Java applets in HTTP traffic from any source to any destination with the following command:

   ciscoasa(config)# **filter java 80 0 0 0 0**

4. (in this configuration, 80 represents HTTP traffic, the first two zeros represent any source (the host who initiated the connection) IP address and mask and the second two zeros represent any destination (the website) IP address and mask)

5. Clear your browser's cache. (In Internet Explorer, you can do this by going to Tools>>Internet Options and deleting your browsing history. In Firefox, you can do this by going to Tools>>Options>>Privacy and clicking the link to clear your recent history.)

6. Refresh the applet page. The Java applet should no longer function.

7. Right-click in a blank area of the page and choose View Source or View Page Source. Note that the Java applet has been commented out by the firewall.

   You can perform similar procedures to filter ActiveX content.

8. Now that you have made additional changes to your configuration, back it up using the procedures learned previously:

   ```
   ciscoasa# copy run tftp://[YOUR PC's IP ADDRESS]/config_filtering.txt
   ```

Hands-On Exercise 11.1: Viewing and Changing the Mode

You must first enable transparent mode on the firewall. Before executing this command, ensure that you have a good backup of the existing configuration. This command will obliterate the existing configuration.

1. In configuration mode, execute the command firewall transparent:

   ```
   ciscoasa# conf t
   ciscoasa(config)# firewall transparent
   ```

2. Next, assign physical interfaces to VLANs using the switchport access command and enable the physical interfaces with the no shutdown command:

   ```
   ciscoasa(config)# interface Ethernet 0/0
   ciscoasa(config-if)# switchport access vlan 2
   ciscoasa(config-if)# no shutdown
   ciscoasa(config-if)# interface Ethernet 0/1
   ciscoasa(config-if)# switchport access vlan 1
   ciscoasa(config-if)# no shutdown
   ```

3. After configuring the physical interfaces, you must configure the VLAN interfaces by giving them names and assigning them to the same bridge-group:

   ```
   ciscoasa(config-if)# interface vlan 2
   ciscoasa(config-if)# nameif outside
   INFO: Security level for "outside" set to 0 by default.
   ciscoasa(config-if)# bridge-group 1
   ciscoasa(config-if)# interface vlan 1
   ciscoasa(config-if)# nameif inside
   INFO: Security level for "inside" set to 100 by default.
   ciscoasa(config-if)# bridge-group 1
   ```

   (Notice that the ASA automatically assigns security levels based on the names inside and outside. If you choose to give the VLAN interfaces different names than inside and outside, you will have to manually assign a security-level of 100 to the inside interface and 0 to the outside interface.)

4. Now, you'll configure the management IP address through the Bridge Virtual Interface (BVI):

   ```
   ciscoasa(config-if)# interface bvi 1
   ciscoasa(config-if)# ip address 192.168.1.240
   ```

   (Notice that I didn't explicitly assign a subnet mask to the BVI's IP address. The ASA can assign a default mask based on the class of the IP address. Since 192.168.1.240 is a Class C address, the ASA automatically assigns a 24-bit mask of 255.255.255.0. If you're using something other than a default subnet mask, you can specify it in dotted-decimal notation following the IP address.)

5. The transparent mode configuration is now complete and the ASA will pass traffic. If you want to use the graphical ASDM (Adaptive Security Device Manager) to manage the device, you must enable the HTTP server and specify which hosts are permitted to access the ASDM with the following commands:

   ```
   ciscoasa(config-if)# http server enable
   ciscoasa(config)# http 0.0.0.0 0.0.0.0 inside
   ```

The first command does what the syntax implies, it enables the server. The second command permits any host connected to the inside interface, regardless of its IP address, to use the HTTP server. You might want to narrow the address range by specifying either your network address (in this example, it would be 192.168.1.0 255.255.255.0) or the host address of your management workstation.

Support and Online Resources

Technical Support

If you require individual technical support, I recommend that you purchase a Cisco SMARTnet contract from the reseller where you purchased your ASA. The SMARTnet contract is not very expensive and it provides you with access to Cisco engineers to help with configuration and troubleshooting.

Online Support

Alternatively, there are a variety of forums where you can post questions and get answers from the community including https://supportforums.cisco.com, http://serverfault.com, and www.experts-exchange.com. Also, consider participating in a Cisco users group. This link will take you to the Cisco Learning Network where you can find resources for getting involved with the Cisco community: https://learningnetwork.cisco.com/welcome

My YouTube channel has a variety of videos showing how to perform common configuration tasks: www.youtube.com/soundtraining. My blog The Accidental Administrator® contains a variety of configuration guides as well: www.accidentaladministrator.com

I also encourage you to subscribe to my email newsletter to receive a notification whenever I add new videos, blog posts, or other learning resources. You can subscribe at www.soundtraining.net/newsletter

Building Your IT Career

Building a successful IT career involves more than just technical knowledge. You must also know how to successfully interact with other people, including bosses, colleagues, and customers. The Compassionate Geek® is a series of books, videos, and workshops designed to help you master the human side of technology. It's all about people skills for tech people. You can learn more at my blog at www.compassionategeek.com and my website at www.doncrawley.com. Also, check out my video channel at www.youtube.com/doncrawley.

Books for IT Pros

For my latest books for IT pros, please visit my Amazon author's page. You'll find it at www.amazon.com/author/doncrawley.

Errors

I wish I could tell you that there are no errors in this lab manual. I've worked really hard to ensure its accuracy, but I'm sure I've missed some errors. If you find errors, first check the errata pages at www.soundtraining.net/bookstore/errata. If you don't see anything there, please send me an email at don@soundtraining.net to let me know what you found.

Thank you for using this lab manual!

Copyright 2016, soundtraining.net. All rights reserved. It is illegal to make copies of this document in any form. www.soundtraining.net If you believe this is an illegal copy, please contact soundtraining.net at (206) 988-5858.

DON R. CRAWLEY
PROFESSIONAL SPEAKER

THE COMPASSIONATE GEEK®

Customer Service Skills for Tech People

DON CRAWLEY

works with tech people who need to improve their customer service skills.

HOW TO BE A COMPASSIONATE GEEK

Success strategies for you and your IT staff

- Improve collaboration and productivity
- Implement the five principles of IT customer service
- Develop emotional intelligence skills
- Learn solid skills for dealing with difficult customers
- Build excellent listening skills
- Uncover ways to show you care
- Master communication through email and other text-based communication tools
- Learn how to say "no" without alienating your end user
- Learn how to manage your stress

WHAT CLIENTS HAVE TO SAY:

"Don was very approachable and helpful ... He knew the material well and seemed to personally be interested and into it."

—Facebook, Navid Mansourian

"Don was able to really help focus our IT team on service delivery by providing tools, concepts and stories that enabled our highly qualified group to excel even more—delivering clear and obvious business value."

—American Superconductor, Michael P. Richardson

"Excellent job. It really got me thinking about my customers and found areas where I can improve myself."

—Discover Card, Elizabeth Vera

"The results were fantastic immediately ... watching three of my team members who were struggling with the very topics you were touching on ... They went out to the client they'd had a difficult interaction with and immediately resolved it."

—National Institutes of Health (NIAMS), Jeffrey Whitehead

"Don is an excellent public speaker and his knowledge of the subject was superb, after all he did write the book on the topic."

—TrainSignal, Kasia Lorenc

"If you're interested in learning from a down-to-earth guy who knows what he's talking about, consider Don Crawley."

—WideOrbit, Paul Nicholson

PROGRAMS

IN PERSON

How to Be a Compassionate Geek (20 to 60 minutes)

Customer Service, Compassion and Computers: Making Them Work Together to Enhance Customer Relationships (3 to 12 hours)

ONLINE

How to Be a Compassionate Geek (60 to 90 minutes)

MEMBER
NSA®
NATIONAL SPEAKERS ASSOCIATION

CRAWLEY INTERNATIONAL, INC.

Don Crawley knows IT customer service. He's the author of *The Compassionate Geek®* series of books on IT customer service. He has spoken to audiences worldwide on the art of serving end users, and he has worked with workplace technology for more than 40 years. Don is a lifetime geek, plus a veteran communicator, based in the global tech hub of Seattle, Washington.

Don R. Crawley, *Professional Speaker*
(206) 988-5858 • don@doncrawley.com
www.doncrawley.com
Seattle, Washington USA

Made in the USA
San Bernardino, CA
21 September 2016